SPIRITUALITY 101

FOR THE DROPOUTS OF THE SCHOOL OF LIFE

THE REVIEW FOR OUR FINAL EXAM

Iván Figueroa-Otero, MD

CREDITS

Author: Iván Figueroa Otero, MD
www.ivanfigueroaoteromd.com
Editor: Yasmín Rodríguez, The Writing Ghost®, Inc.
Translation: The Writing Ghost®, Inc.
www.thewritingghost.com
Cover design: Gil Acosta Design
www.gilacosta.com
Photography: Emmanuel Berríos
Book setup and production: The Writing Ghost®, Inc.

ISBN-13: 978-0-9964666-6-0
Número de la Librería del Congreso: 2017905674

First Edition, 2014
Second Edition, 2021
Part of Dr. Figueroa's series:
"School of Life"

REVIEWS FOR SPIRITUALITY 101

"In his debut, the author captivates the reader with a composition [that is] very easy to read, encouraging the reader to 'scrutinize the concept that life is a prison created by the bars of his own mind.' Its elegant and striking design is full of reliefs and colorful illustrations to emphasize the most important parts of the content. The author presents many explanations with a jocular irony, which makes his reading pleasant."

Kirkus Book Review

"Dr. Iván Figueroa Otero writes a very persuasive book on how to live in a spiritual world, in a way so easy to understand that it is elegant in its simplicity."

Joslyn Wolfe, Focus on Women Magazine

"An immediate sales success with great reviews from its readers, this book is a Finalist at the 2014 National Indie Excellence Awards. —Your book is a true example of the excellence these awards celebrate, and we pay tribute to you and your great work."

National Indie Review

"Spirituality 101 is a book for people who want to better understand the world in which they live. It is a book about life and how human beings can reconcile the apparent discrepancy of understanding life between science and religious traditions. No matter your religious vision, this book teaches you to live in balance within this existential paradox. The author achieves this reconciliation through a format of school lessons to be applied at the School of Life."

Samantha Rivera, Reader's Favorite

Comment from a reader:

"Congratulations! I met you during one of the most intense lessons of my life, and I saw in you a Warrior of Light, a Winner. From that moment, whenever I remember it, my heart thanks and congratulates you. God will continue to bless you."

Álida Castro Marrero

OTHER BOOKS BY THE AUTHOR

Spirituality 1.2

For The Disconnected from the School of Life

A Review for Tekkies Tekkies

Spirituality 103

Key to Forgiveness

Finding the Light in Our Shadows

Spirituality 104

Reflections in my Magical Mirror

Lessons of Love from the School of Life

IMAGE ON THE COVER: FRACTALS

Fractals are mathematical models of repetitive geometric structures. Many natural systems are of a fractal type because nature tends to repeat geometric and mathematical sequences. For my part, I think the repetition of shapes occurring from the macrocosm (visible and measurable by our senses) down to the microcosm (invisible and unmeasurable) seems to establish a common (holographic) link between all parts of the universe, as described in this book.

DEDICATION

I dedicate this book to all teachers, students, and patients who participate with me in the School of Life, and who inspired me to share all of their experiences and lessons. Especially my patients who, with the testimonials of their lessons of love, helped me find the Key to Forgiveness to reach the healing code of the soul. Without them, my academic progress in the universal classroom would not have been possible.

If, while being reflected by this book's mirror, some of you rediscover your shadow-distorted light, share the merit of the results with your fellow students, as well as the learning that follows from reading it.

TABLE OF CONTENTS

ACKNOWLEDGEMENTS

Among all the travelers that have shared this endless journey in the reflection of my Mind's Magical Mirror, I want to particularly thank my children, their mother and my patient wife Ivette, who have supported this old man's follies with so much affection.

I especially appreciate the spiritual guidance from my Masters in the Nyingma Tibetan Buddhist tradition, the Venerable Khenchen Palden Sherab Rinpoche and Khenpo Tsewang Dongyal Rinpoche, from whom I learned a good portion of the mental training that allowed me to write about the wonderful wisdom of the Mirror of our minds.

I equally acknowledge the primordial influence that the six volumes of Ser Uno (Being One), www.elseruno.com, channeled by its author/channeler (anonymous), had over this book.

Finally, my thanks to my Mother, Doña Berta, for hours spent reading the Christian Bible during my childhood, assuring me that at some point it would strengthen me during the difficult times in my life.

"The Master is nothing more than a disciple, who likes to help others find their mastery."

"The weapons of the true Warrior of Light are compassion and the patience to wait for the other person to learn what he has already learned."

Iván Figueroa-Otero, MD

SOLITUDE

Loneliness is a conceptual state, not a situational state.

It is a psychic deprivation or alienation of our primordial loving nature,

Which potentially resides in every sentient being in the Universe.

Yet, it still exists within the clamorous effervescence of crowds.

Paradoxically, that feeling of isolation disappears spontaneously when we penetrate the solace of our inner silence,

Which makes us feel complete and satisfied by the purest essence of Love.

After having tried this indescribable delicacy, a new way to look at the infinitely variable manifestations of apparent reality emerges,

3

Which allows us to observe them without judging their

illusory purposes

and results.

This new vision, born of our own heart and all the

beings

of this Universe, dissolves all

vestige of suffering away from our being,

When we understand that Happiness has always been

with us

on this path without beginning or end.

Iván Figueroa Otero

"DROPOUTS" VS. DROPOUTS

In the traditional school, a dropout is a student that flunked his exams and left school. But, at the School of Life, flunking does not mean failing. It is more of a learning experience that is not completed yet since the options for repeating the lessons never run out.

At the School of Life, there are no grades or organized curriculum. Everyone comes to learn and progress in particular areas, and the lessons are structured by daily life. It is as if the curriculum is created while you study. Each experience becomes a new opportunity to grow and develop integrally. Each person decides when they learned sufficiently to move to the next course.

Who, then, are the dropouts in the School of Life? They are the ones who are not satisfied with their lives. For some reason, they are frustrated, stressed, insecure, or sad and may feel they have failed in some progress issues. In these cases, students will repeat the experiences until they overcome the blockage to continue progressing.

Fully graduating from the School of Life is a human being's most important process. The issue is that, in that process, you get the exams the same day you receive the lesson! That is why, when we fail, things get more challenging because the next day's test will include the material from the previous one. People who quit without realizing that they can repeat the test forever are boycotting themselves when they stop trying to pass it.

I am one of those life dropouts that repeated many subjects. Through that experience, I learned how to facilitate passing the exams (which are about overcoming life experiences). This book is one of many that are coming out to help the dropouts and should not be approached as the only way to progress in life.

Like other schools, the School of Life ascends in levels as we awaken to the experience of living. In this school, the teacher-student roles are not well defined since students of all grade levels share the classroom of life. This educational system is based on an infinite amount of levels where the most advanced students teach the lower classes and learn from the upper ones.

Suppose the School of Life is full of dropouts. *In that case,* as is happening during these times, advanced-level graduates return and share their wisdom with lower-level groups to help them pass the corresponding exams. These lagging students perhaps were the "poor in spirit," the holy scriptures referred to and those that Jesus considered when he spoke to his Father and said, "Father, forgive them because they do not know what they are doing." (Lucas 23:34.)

The topics covered in this review are based on how I interpreted life lessons in class and how they might guide others on their respective paths in the School of Life's infinite hierarchy.

These classes' topics are divided into four phases: life as a social, family, professional and spiritual being. We will explore how spirituality helps guide students in each of these phases to manifest the best outcome.

I want to express my heartfelt appreciation to all who became my teachers at every stage of my experiences and helped me better understand my life lessons. My wholehearted apologies to those who, in my ignorance, I caused some discomfort in my learning process.

I must clarify that this book is not a book of religion but spirituality, where I attempt to explain that difference. I will use tools from all faiths to facilitate understanding of the spiritual concepts that bind all religions but will abstain from talking about those that separate them. I wish that this text becomes one of the many messages prepared by life itself for our enjoyment in universal love.

This second edition is a new effort to simplify the message, clarify the topics discussed, and enlarge the font size. And, sadly, the funny emoticons had to go.

I hope that, by the end of this book, you will be able to answer your version of the archetypal questions of our lives: Who am I? Where do I come from? And where am I going? As described in the introductory poem, you may find the origin of our happiness resides within us since the beginning of our infinite and collective cosmic experience. Let us begin this lesson of love with a joyful heart.

THE ORIGIN OF THE UNIVERSE

Glossary - Chapter I

The "Big Bang"—This is the scientific community's mainstream hypothesis to explain the origin of our universe. It postulates that the cosmos originated from a point of mass densification or singularity, where nothing existed, but everything would emerge eventually (what?). Do not feel bad if you did not understand it, because even the experts disagree! From this silent explosion, progressively and expansively, our universe manifested itself in all its magnificent splendor. Since then, similarly, many scientific minds have exploded, trying to understand this phenomenon!

Antimatter—The opposite of matter, that science postulates existed in equal proportion to matter after the "Big Bang," but that scientists have lost track of ever since. It is believed to produce matter, but scientists do not know how (do you see how precise and accurate science is?). Today, antimatter is almost non-existent for the objective measures of our instruments.

Dark Energy—An energy known to exist because it influences matter, which takes up much of the universe's space (72%), but that has never been seen or measured (Believe it by faith!).

Dark Matter— The matter that occupies the other 23% of the universe, although we know nothing of it, except for its influence on gravity.

Matter—That which composes our understandable, measurable, and visible universe, being the 5% in which we seem to live.

Hologram—Three-dimensional projection obtained from a flat image created by laser techniques. Today, it is used on television to send a person's tridimensional image to distant places. Soon we will see this technology in our homes. The important thing is to understand that Dr. Bhom, a scientist, established that the entire original could be reproduced from any part of an object in the universe. This suggests that the whole image's information is contained within each of its parts and that a form of intrinsic communication exists between all of them.

Dimension—The way we perceive how we exist within space (three dimensions: width, length and depth or height), plus the perception of time. Not all animals observe the universe this way. For example, ants only see two dimensions and do not perceive height (is that why they do not fall off walls?). Being able to observe a three-dimensional universe depends on our binocular vision and how our brain processes it. When we lose the vision of one eye we lose three-dimensional sight, but not that of the other senses (yet the blind can read the three-dimensional figures of Braille with their fingers).

Time—It is a very subjective definition of the observer's experience when they interpret a series of events with the five senses and, based on the brain's capacity, divide them into imaginary segments of present, past, and future. To determine the weather, we use references to observable changes in the seasons (climates) and the cycles of day and night. Based on these changes, humans divided time into sections of seconds, minutes, hours, days, months, years, centuries, etc. (Now you understand why it is so difficult to get to appointments on time!).

Einstein's theory of relativity—This theory explains how time is interpreted differently from place to place in the Universe. It states that the maximum speed that a material particle or object can obtain in the cosmos is the speed of light, and that the faster the particle goes, the slower the passage of time and aging will be experienced. This would imply that when a particle reaches the speed of light, its time stops and disappears for us in our three-dimensional perception of time (we will refer to this later, so remember it.)

14

Love—an immeasurable dormant state, from which all possibilities of manifestation of life exist and from where they all originate, including the consciousness of perceiving it in all its infinite and contrasting appearances. It is the light and sound that existed before the "Big Bang," just like they exist at night, before dawn. Its archetypical qualities are infinite patience, equanimity, understanding and tolerance, which allows its offspring the use of free will. These qualities join all parts of creation in a in a skein or tapestry, woven by the unwavering force of love (I am who I am).

HOW DID WE GET INTO THIS MESS?

This chapter's main lesson is an attempt to answer the questions that most humans ask themselves at some point in their lives: Where do I come from? Who am I? Where am I going? To answer them, we must cautiously delve into the realm of science. Please, do not panic because I will hold your hand the whole way.

And in the beginning, there was only love. And in her dream, love saw all the possibilities of creation, and a tremendous explosion awakened her. When she opened her eyes, she was no longer alone!

Because of the discrepancies in the stories about the universe's creation from the main religions throughout history, and because of my lack of knowledge, I have focused my discussion on the information that science provides us and my interpretation of that.

It is interesting to share that my analysis of the scientific vision of the universe and the cosmological teachings of Buddhism brought me back to my Christian roots. While I was studying other religious concepts, I understood better those of my upbringing.

The most accepted theory of the formation of the universe is that of the "Big Bang." This theory postulates that everything appeared from a singular point where it existed in a dormant state, which manifested in an enormous explosion that created a

16

universe that is still expanding at present. Initially, this universe's structure had equal parts of matter (50% - what we see and believe we are) and antimatter (50% - what we do not perceive and don't know what it is).

In some way unknown to science, antimatter was reduced to an unmeasurable amount, which we know exists but cannot perceive. Then, two new components appeared: dark energy (72%) and dark matter (23%), which may be the measurable manifestation of antimatter. *If we add both 72% + 23% = 95%, it suggests that the universe we live in (matter) is only 5% of the total!*

According to our human senses and scientific instruments, matter is predominant. But, that is an illusion because when we add the lost percentages of antimatter, it's clear we only perceive and understand 5% of our universe. No wonder there are so many troubled people on our planet!

This perceptible percentage creates a paradox: it seems we have been deceived by the misunderstanding that humans are the center of this universe and the culminating work of creation! (Don't panic yet. Later, I will give you information that will boost your self-esteem again.) So, why don't we perceive all those other portions of our universe? In an attempt to understand, we must divide our universe into two parts: one that we perceive with our senses of vision, touch, smell, hearing, and taste, and one that we can not perceive at all.

The capabilities of these senses vary from animal to animal. Some animal's senses (yes, we are animals, some a little more than others!) are superior or inferior to ours, which implies that we do not perceive it the same way although we share the same universe.

Our awareness of the universe is the sum of what we experience with all our senses plus the interpretation we learned during our process of socialization, parenting, education, and hereditary tendencies. This implies that our personality is similar to a program (software) influenced by what we have learned in our lives and the inherited characteristics of our parents (we will go into more detail about this in other chapters).

Our universe is like the moon's reflection on a lake

Imagine the surprise of the human precursors when they first observed the moon's reflection on a body of calm water without knowing the source of the image. Similarly, humans detect only the material reflection of the source, antimatter, that our senses perceive as our reality, like a holographic image of the initial universal hologram.

This hologram is a tridimensional illusion that, together with the perceived relativity of time, becomes an emotional trap that imprisons us in the fantasy of birth and death that makes us feel the emotions of fear, suffering, and pain, and does not let us remember our natural origin.

Imagine this idea of the universe like an excellent theater play with multiple scripts where we have many roles. When we meet our fellow actors after a performance, we talk about the quality of the acting and how we can improve it.

To find our home, we must look at the stars and find the source of the explosion, not the image reflected in the surface of the lake, created by our five senses.

Are we children of love (God), or children of man?

Scientifically, as Carl Sagan put it, we are children of the stars because we are composed of cosmic dust that originated after the "Big Bang." This scientific fact makes us carriers of a common lineage that then became human DNA, the hereditary material that originated life on our planet.

No matter our race, color, or gender, we all come from that first DNA. Since we have already established that matter manifested itself only as 5% of our reality and that the rest of the universe (the other 95%) originated from the same source, we must conclude that we have a common lineage. This seems to imply that our origin is dual in nature, where we are children of love (God-antimatter) and children of man (matter-time).

If we understand that biological DNA stores the memories of everything that has manifested in our matter from the "Big Bang," we should be able to accept that the rest of the universe, the antimatter, must also have a memory or recording in its antimaterial (spiritual) DNA. For now, let us only accept that we are creatures with a dual manifestation, as children of God and children of man, with a common genealogy, no matter our race, sex, or religion.

Science also splits the universe into two parts according to its scientific explanation: the universe ruled by the laws of Newtonian physics, which defines the behavior of material objects on a visible, large scale, and the universe of quantum physics, which explains the laws of behavior of invisible, smaller parts in the subatomic world. In the first interpretation, 2 + 2 is always 4, but in the second vision the result is only one of many probabilities or solutions.

In quantum physics, nothing is impossible – just more or less probable. The observer's thoughts influence the manifestation of what is observed.

Do you see how the intention of our thoughts is so important? Look at the next chart.

CLASSIC PHYSICS (Material Universe - 5%)	QUANTUM PHYSICS (Antimatter Universe - 95%)
It's deterministic:	It's probabilistic:
If we know an object's position and velocity, we	You can never know with absolute certainty what

can determine where it is going.	something will turn into. It cannot be reproduced since it varies depending on the interpretation of the observer.
It's reductionist: The parts of this universe seem to act independently from others.	It's holistic: The universe is a unified holographic whole, whose parts instantaneously interact with each other.
The observers perceive the universe as something outside themselves and do not feel like they are part of it. Reality is external and independent of the observer.	The observers are an interdependent part of their universe. They are a microcosm of their macrocosm and maintain a holographic relationship with the whole. They can change the universe with their thoughts.

It applies to the visible world on a large scale, but not to the subatomic world.	Applicable to every invisible antimatter scale in the universe, since everything that's visible is also composed of subatomic particles.
It's based on the knowledge of "absolute truths or laws." Time is absolute everywhere in the universe. The universe is tridimensional.	It's based on the knowledge of a universe that changes continually in infinite cycles with "tendencies to exist" or "tendencies to happen". Time is relative everywhere in the universe depending on the object's and observer's speed (law of relativity). The universe is multidimensional.

The development of modern science was primarily influenced by the dualist philosophy postulated by the Cartesian theory, which, using the mechanical basis of Isaac Newton's physics, stated: "I think. Therefore, I am." Descartes proposed that the process of knowledge and learning should be limited to the world of rational and scientific analysis based on laws established by the use of the five senses (if I can't perceive it, it does not exist).

Humanity's material side seemed to be independent of the one that seemed to live beyond its physical aspect, referred to as metaphysics – something that cannot be measured, therefore unknowable according to scientific laws. The study of metaphysics seemed to lay outside the realm of reason. A dualist vision of the human being emerged, where the metaphysical (spirit) or transcendental had no importance or influence on its material part.

This idea prevailed in science until the development of quantum physics and Einstein's theory of relativity at the beginning of the 20th century. These new theories began to determine the existence of a subatomic, invisible universe, apart from absolute time and the possible presence of dimensions beyond the three traditional ones. (This caused a scientific "free for all" that is still happening).

For the first time, the metaphysical universe was established as a multidimensional or transcendental (antimatter) aspect of reality. Based on this new knowledge, I suggest that we should change the Cartesian axiom: "I think, therefore I am," to "I am, therefore I think." **Matter originated after the "Big Bang" from the antimatter, which in turn developed from an indefinable potential point, which I characterize as love. That is why I refer to the "Big Bang" as the "Great Explosion of Love."**

God's description of himself in the Bible supports this statement. On Mount Sinai, at Moses' insistence (in one of the many translated versions of **"Ehyeh asher Ehyeh"**), he replies, "I am who I am" (Exodus

3:14), which I convert to the impersonal form: "I am what I am." or "I will be what I will be." It means that whatever It needs to be, he can become. This shows the indefinable and inclusive nature of Its greatness, which lovingly adjusts to what His children need Him to be for them, and the potential of His creative force that inherently existed before the Big Explosion of Love ("Big Bang").

Summing it up, the universe seems to originate from a single point where the great explosion of love (God) manifested in countless forms of antimatter (Spirit, dark matter, dark energy). These, in turn, manifest themselves as matter in the dual structure of the Children of God (invisible) within the Children of Man (visible, Christ), forming the universal trinity, or the triangle of love.

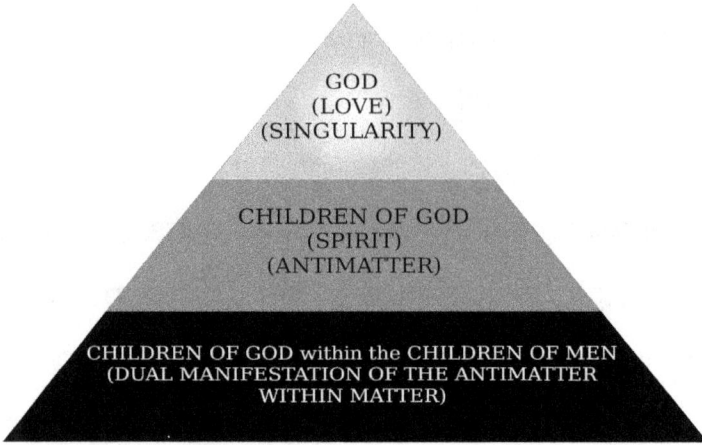

GOD
(LOVE)
(SINGULARITY)

CHILDREN OF GOD
(SPIRIT)
(ANTIMATTER)

CHILDREN OF GOD within the CHILDREN OF MEN
(DUAL MANIFESTATION OF THE ANTIMATTER
WITHIN MATTER)

Shared responsibility (co-responsibility) and shared creativeness (co-creation) are two qualities that should govern us in our universal journey

To understand these concepts, we must review what we read previously.

In defining our universe as a holographic and quantum model, we must remember that the inexorable matrix of love entirely interconnects it. Since each of its parts belongs to the same family or lineage of antimatter (Spirit), no matter how distant or different we perceive ourselves in the material planes of time and space, we are always interconnected in love. What occurs in a part of a hologram still affects all its components.

These Bible quotes confirm this, "[…] *Truly I tell you, whatever you did for one of the least of these brothers and sisters of mine, you did for me."* (Mathew 25:40), *"Love your neighbor as yourself"* (Mark 12:31), and the Golden Rule, *"Do to others what you would have them to do to you,"* (Mathew 7:12.)

These quotes convey that the Golden Rule binds our common universal lineage and all its parts. From this awareness comes the understanding of how our free will, used irresponsibly (innocently?), can create suffering in others and ourselves. In another chapter, I will try to explain how the law of love corrects imbalances caused by the irresponsible actions of its children.

Co-creation comes from the observer's ability to perceive the universe in all the infinite possibilities offered by the hologram while carefully learning to use our free will to understand the good, the bad, and the ugly within the magnificence of our lives.

This critical way of seeing the universe traps the human (Children of Man). They are not aware that they are also Children of God (quantum being), in their self-created emotional prison by the selfishness of its ego. We already know that any mental action in the holographic quantum world affects the universe around it, creating a reaction throughout the hologram. This response is the result we refer to as our co-responsibility and co-creation of that mental action.

That is why we must always base how we intend to observe our universe on the common lineage of love. The only way love can manifest itself in the universe is through the Sons of Man, recognizing the unifying bond of our spiritual heritage as sons and daughters of God.

Let us answer the questions that started our chapter:

Where do I come from?

We are children of the Great Explosion of Love that produced the entire universe. We carry a common lineage that unites us in its endless matrix, which manifests itself in all the different and infinite dimensions, allowing us to participate in this infinite co-creation with an attitude of loving co-responsibility.

Who am I?

I am a creature of light (love), with countless dimensional manifestations in shades of love and life. Our transient experiences within matter, time, and space (human beings) reside in these manifestations, allowing me to use my free will in a co-responsible manner in the co-creation process.

Do you understand now why we cannot blame others for our failures and suffering?

HOMEWORK

Practice finding the other 95% of our universe.

1. Observe all that surrounds us with our five
    senses. Can we see, smell, feel, hear, and taste
    everything we know exists? We know we cannot.
    Let us think about things we know exist but
    cannot perceive.

    a) Have we ever seen the wind that moves
       three's branches?

    b) Has anyone seen or felt X-rays when they are
       taken, or seen or felt the infinite and invisible
       emissions of the sun's rays that incessantly
       penetrate our bodies?

    c) Have we ever seen the unceasing thoughts
       that our minds generate?

    d) Can someone tell us precisely where the
       mind exists and describe its configuration?

e) Can we precisely locate where our emotions happen?

f) Do we see all the millions of microscopic and submicroscopic organisms that live throughout the surface of our bodies?

Looking at the body externally, we cannot see all the types of cells that compose themselves organs. No one questions their reality, yet we believe in their existence based on scientific evidence.

These simple observations make us understand that not everything that exists is perceivable by our senses. Are you able to understand, now, where is the rest of the universe?

2. Look around, notice everything you see, and find its origin. See if you can smell, touch, taste, or hear your thoughts and those of others. Try to see or hear the electrical currents that create the nerve conduction of those thoughts. Feel the surface of your bodies and the objects around

you. Notice its texture, solidity, and elasticity. Look at your hands and understand that they are composed of muscle tissue, cartilage, and bone, which in turn are composed of invisible cells, molecules, and organic compounds and are ultimately made of invisible subatomic particles.

3. All other parts of your body are made up of the same elementary particles. But why do we see them so differently? How did we learn to differentiate our universe? Are the names assigned to these qualities the same for all languages? Notice how, throughout your lives, your actions have influenced others, their environment, and their present situation.

4. Now, meditate silently on what you observed previously and answer: Where is my visible self or individuality? Where is my invisible part? If you find it, email me, and tell me where it is!

BONUS QUESTIONS TO IMPROVE YOUR GRADE

1. If the "Big Bang" occurred from a singularity, where everything was still in preexistence and a condensed potential state: where did the preexisting stuff come from?

2. Why do I say the explosion was silent?

3. Why do I refer to love as feminine? Study the Yin and Yang theory.

4. Why, if we are all children of God, made in his image and likeness, we do not all manifest love in the universe? Review Jesus' sentence from his last moments: "Father, forgive them, for they do not know what they are doing." (Luke 23:34). And we could add, "for they have forgotten that they are your children and my brethren in the love of the Spirit."

5. Suppose the process of interpreting, understanding, investigating, and reasoning only happens with less than 5% of the data. Could

35

anyone say they have the absolute truth? What position should we assume when we disagree with others about the way we understand life?

6. How many possible visions of what God means to man can exist?

AS RIVERS OF THE GREAT OCEAN:

THE FALSE PERCEPTION OF INDIVIDUALISM AND SEPARATION

Glossary - Chapter II

The Law of Conservation of Energy – The first law of thermodynamics, which states that energy cannot be created or destroyed, but can only be transformed from one form to another. E.g., Energy <> matter in an infinite bidirectional way. It seems this universe will never end!

Qi or Chi– A term used in the Chinese medical eastern tradition, to refer to a power that may be in higher vibratory states (energy) or lower or denser (matter).

Ego– In Latin, it means the Self. In this text, it refers to the Self, which makes us feel as individuals and observers of the universe around us (individualism). It allows us to perceive what is ours and what belongs to others, to observe the effects of time (being born, aging, getting sick and dying), and to interpret our quality of life through the emotions generated by our five senses, categorizing them into good or bad experiences. Our personality comes from these experiences.

Selfishness– A way to live in the universe based on independence and individualism that makes us feel falsely separated in races, colors, religions, knowledge, and power, where our actions and their effects are not observed as interdependent. (It is the world of mine and yours and not ours!)

Personality– Programming (software) that led us to believe it defines who we are. It comes from a combination of the hereditary characteristics of both parents, the experiences acquired or learned from our parents, friends, teachers, religions, books, social environment, and the media.

Transcendent– That which by its nature transcends the physical experience, which some people call metaphysical. It refers to the antimaterial universe, where the concepts of time and space do not exist.

Periodic Table–The one I call "The Great Symphony of the Chemical Elements." It is the arranging of the elements into groups based on their atomic number, which classifies them into families with different chemical characteristics.

"The Universe is like a great ocean of Qi in which we are like rivers that drain into it. At any given moment, we may believe that we are only individual rivers, but when we merge with the ocean, we realize that we were never separated from it. Some of us emerge as broad and turbulent rivers. Others, as tranquil or as weak streams, but we were never alone on our paths. Whatever affects the ocean affects the river, and what affects the river impacts the ocean."

—Iván Figueroa Otero MD

Let's review the previous chapter and remember that the Self appeared as a dual manifestation made in God's image after the Great Explosion of Love. This dual Self showcases the qualities of the Children of God (Spirit-antimatter) and the Children of Man (matter-time-space).

We must remember that the physical universe in which human beings exist only occupies 5% of the entire universe. This portion is governed by the laws of classical physics (check the table in the previous chapter), where time affects their experience by the cycles of birth and death occurring in the physical form of life.

Also, from the previous chapter, we can understand the paradox created by the apparent duality of a temporal being who lives in the time and habits created by his mind, suggesting that life begins at birth and ends with death. But, does something really die in this universe? Are birth and death only infinite transformations of energy to matter and vice versa, as Einstein demonstrates in his theory of relativity? (Law of Conservation of Energy) The universe is the most efficient recycling factory that exists, so we must be careful not to be recycled too soon!

It is unreasonable to believe that we cease to exist because 5% of our body disappears from the material world. However, it is worth asking, where was the other 95% of my being before birth, and where does it go when my body dies? Will we knowingly accept that our awareness will disappear with our ashes?

Referring to the poem at the beginning of this chapter, we must ask: Why do the rivers lose awareness of their original ocean? This apparent separation of the Children of Man (time and matter) from their source, God (antimatter, timeless), originates with the emergence of the concept of self (ego) when the biological organism develops the five senses.

Scientific studies highlight that the process of observing the external universe through the five senses is a very subjective process of interpretation and organization, in which we arrange the visible world by accepting what others have previously experienced.

These learned patterns that govern our lives become good or bad habits, depending on how they make us feel.

It is like when, to put a puzzle together, we have to see the final image. It would be almost impossible to assemble one without that reference. Similarly, it is the concordance in repeated experiences that leads us to establish the social paradigms that allow us to live together in civilized social structures. These experiences vary depending on their geographical and racial influence.

42

The outside world looks, smells, tastes, feels, and is heard more with the brain than with the outer senses. We will see later how quantum physics suggests that the observer influences the manifestation of the observed and that how we experience our external reality will vary depending on the lessons or habits learned during the process of living.

Our realities vary depending on the color of the lens we use to observe them, influenced by what we learned and inherited. (Beauty is in the eye of the beholder.)

Independence versus Interdependence: Individualism's False Impression

Individualism originates from the apparent experience of birth and physical dissolution (death) of the temporal manifestation of our bodies. That transition generates the concept of time, aging, disease, and the urgency to take advantage of the experience that we call life.

On the basis that they must make efficient use of their time, humans decide to seek what satisfies them and bring them happiness without considering their effects on others who share their experience. This rampant individualism is the origin of selfishness (ego). It produces the hedonistic lifestyle described in Ricky Martin's song "La Vida Loca." The people who live in this fashion can never really find happiness.

The pursuit of happiness is one of the few actions in which human beings agree, even if they disagree on what it means and how to find it. This quest for satisfaction emphasizes creating physical and mental boundaries that we would like to "privatize," or fence in, for our well-being and security, trying to keep them immutable in their appearance and action. Finally, that quest becomes insatiable and only ends in more suffering and dissatisfaction.

The result of this search is the endless cycle of the changes that generate time and the time that produces change. (Dwell on this paradox for a while!)

44

Origins of Suffering

Humans who do not understand where they come from and who they really are feel lost in an endless battle with time and the changes they created with their habits. They also have a discrepancy with others about what happiness really is.

Living, if we do it with selfishness and lack of awareness of our interdependence with the universal laws and other beings, becomes a nightmare of suffering with brief moments of happiness (it feels like a soap opera).

Happiness is a state of inner balance (well-being) of the mind, which does not depend on what is going on outside itself.

The Children of Man would seem to have forgotten their true origin, creating a fictional separation from their Creator. Then, to rediscover happiness, we must remember our actual origin and understand that the experience of life is just one, where the transcendental manifests itself in an infinite and changing range of possibilities. Interdependence with others is unavoidable, allowing our humanity's solidarity to appear within this experience. **We will then remember that the origin of all this suffering is ignorance of our true nature.**

All religions emphasized that human beings should understand their spiritual origin to find love and peace in their lives. (History suggests that their followers did not understand the message!)

The Bible stressed that the Kingdom of God was not of this world but, paradoxically, it could be found in the heart of every human. This is consistent with the dual presence of the Self we described previously.

We should understand that humans were the ones who, with their minds, locked themselves in their own self-imposed prison, created by the bars of his selfishness (five senses). Then they forgot how they previously existed in the house of their Creator.

The Speed of Light, the Imaginary Frontier That Divides Time from Non-Time

Einstein proved that time is relative to the speed of light, where time for an observer traveling through space would seem to slow down as the speed of the ship increased. In theory, if the ship's velocity could reach the speed of light, time would disappear, and the spaceship would cease to exist for other observers who are traveling in slower vessels.

In this way, a virtual barrier divides the universe into two parts, one visible in time and one invisible for any object that could travel at the speed of light.

All matter in the universe is composed, in its most essential state, by specific configurations of invisible subatomic particles, which in turn are grouped into visible elements and compounds, as happens in the periodic table. We could hypothesize that our bodies have invisible matter (subatomic particles) and visible matter (elements and compounds).

If we accept the scientific theory that most subatomic particles travel near, or at the speed of light, we would have to conclude that they are out of our space-time and are invisible.

And, if we already accept that our bodies are made up of 95% subatomic particles (antimatter), then some of our self is invisible, out of space-time, and immortal! (But, be careful what you do, because the mortal part is an inescapable reality!)

We can conclude that we are multidimensional travelers who share the duality of time and timelessness simultaneously while mainly being aware of our physical Self. In other words, we are the Children of God, living within the Children of Man!

We could conclude that the selfish actions and transgressions of Man stem from the ignorance of their real origin and nature as Children of God ("Father, forgive them, for they do not know what they are doing.")

When men feel like "family", where blood and genetic inheritance is the strength of love, they spontaneously manifest the qualities that have for so long been repressed by their ignorance, fear, and anger. Selfishness then dissipates, with the feeling of being "part of" and not "separate from" your brothers and sister in the light. As said by the Three Musketeers, "All for one and one for all!"

This is how we understand love as described by St Paul in his epistle, "Love is patient, love is kind. It does not envy, it does not boast, it is not proud. It does not dishonor others, it is not self-seeking, it is not easily angered, it keeps no record of wrongs. Love does not delight in evil but rejoices with the truth. It always protects, always trusts, always hopes, always perseveres." (1 Corinthians 13:4-7).

HOMEWORK

Let's review our life's history. Remember the happiest moments. Were those moments related to material achievements, such as honors, diplomas, property, cars, or riches? Or were they less practical events such as weddings, the birth of a child or grandchild, graduation, or the success of a loved one?

How many events achieved from material goals had not-so-pleasant consequences later, such as the responsibility for paying a new car or the mortgage on a home? Did your educational milestones and diplomas bring you what you expected, or did they only add responsibilities and obligations?

Did your financial goals or public recognition prevent the many sad moments of your life, such as the death and illness of a loved one or a divorce in your family? How many cosmetic surgeries do we need to maintain the illusion of eternal youth? No operation can erase the emotional scars in our hearts when we have already aged to the point that we cannot enjoy the simple things in life.

Let's review our lives and remember how many others we owe all our accomplishments to, and let's be grateful to them. It is usually an endless list, starting with our parents. Now let us silently meditate about how all our actions and their consequences have affected others and how others have changed our life. Do we feel like rivers of the Great Ocean or as rivers that follow an unknown course? Let us finish in silent meditation and search again where your Self or your mind is.

BONUS QUESTIONS TO IMPROVE YOUR GRADE

1. If happiness is a state of well-being created by the mind, what should I do about the experiences of suffering in order to mitigate them?

2. Is there evil in humans? If it does not exist, why do we perform actions that create suffering in others?

3. Where can we find love in this conflicting world? (Suggestion: look in your mirror!)

4. What can we do to change the habits learned, which do not let us recognize that we are Children of God and feel loved? (Suggestion: What do we do with obsolete programs on our computer?)

OUR UNIVERSE, A TIMELESS STORY

Glossary - Chapter III

Brain Hemisphere Theory—Neurology and psychology tell us that each brain hemisphere predominates in certain functions. The left hemisphere is associated with reason and logic. It processes information analytically and sequentially, step by step, logically and linearly. This hemisphere analyzes, abstracts, counts, measures time, plans procedures, verbalizes, and thinks in words and numbers. In other words, it can do mathematics, reading, and writing. The right hemisphere is associated with feeling and emotions and specializes in global perception and synthesizing information. With it, we see how the parts combine to form the whole. Thanks to the right hemisphere, we understand metaphors, dream, create music and create new combinations of ideas. It is intuitive and emotional rather than logical, preferring images, symbols, and feelings. It has an imaginative and fantastic ability for spatial and perceptual cognition.

Co-creation—It is the process of creativeness where love (God) facilitates and empowers his children with free will to manifest a universe and makes them responsible for the results. Those results will depend on the loving or selfish intention of God's children.

Cosmic schizophrenia—A state of mental confusion where the Self manifests a double personality, as Children of God or Children of Man, that makes them live in an unbalanced universe and which brings them much confusion and suffering. Most of these believed themselves to be only children of man and consider those who believe to be children of God to be mad.

Free will—The ability of a rational being that, within its capabilities or limitations, chooses the most beneficial option at any given time in its individual experience. Free will is not the same for everyone: it varies according to intelligence, social status, politics, ethics, and personal health. It is associated with the potential of acting with relative freedom. This vision focused on individualism generates extremely independent actions, known as selfishness.

Primordial nature (love)—What existed before the "Big Bang," and the origin of everything. It is the feminine part of the trinity (Yin, or the Spirit) that creates the "Big Bang" (Yang).

Shamata—A meditation technique that aims to calm the mind, focusing it on an object or action. (E.g., candles, statues, activities, music, prayers, mantras, or repetitive acts).

Tower of Babel—A tower that the first Hebrew tribes began to build to reach Heaven (they were homesick), since they all had a universal language that facilitated the process. God, who did not want men to do so, scattered them on the earth and changed their languages so that they would not understand each other and could not finish the tower. (Yahweh was such a trickster!)

RESPONSIBLE CO-CREATION BORN FROM OUR FREE WILL

In this chapter, we will focus on continuing to clarify the question: Who am I?

Our understanding of the universe is like a fairy tale with no beginning or end, where the reader creates the plot as he reads.

In reviewing the first two chapters, we could conclude that we live in a universe of apparent dual manifestations created by how the Self perceives the universe through its five senses. In previous chapters, we discussed the inconvenience of the Self living mostly conscious of only the 5% it perceives. This generates fictitious and conflicting barriers between its two natures that prevent self-understanding, as suggested by the Greek philosophers and the teachings of the Far East.

This person would seem to be living **cosmic schizophrenia,** where those who accompany them along the way consider them normal because they share the same hallucinations! Yet, they feel those who tell them about the invisible world of love to be crazy!

Human Being's Duality

Throughout history, human's dual nature has been the theological basis of almost all existing religions and spiritual philosophies. We could classify it for discussion as:

1. An absolute-imperceptible nature (transcendental, immaterial, invisible, immutable, and immeasurable)

2. A relative-perceptible nature (apparent, material, visible, changing and perishable)

This situation provokes some existential questions. Are we physical beings limited to the laws of time and matter? Are we spiritual beings with a material manifestation independent of their origin? Or are we persons with both qualities manifesting simultaneously, where one or the other predominates from moment to moment, depending on innumerable factors? What I have learned from my multiple failures in the school of life, and after repeating several courses, suggests that an affirmative answer to the last question is the most appropriate.

The problem is that humans are mostly aware of their relative nature only and find it challenging to comprehend their absolute part. These two natures are present in humans in a continuously changing interaction that allows the predominance of one or the other, influenced by these factors:

1. The person's ability to realize these qualities exist. (This is the most critical milestone to pass the final exam of the School of Life)

2. The ability to understand their origin

3. The ability to know how they interact

4. The ability to comprehend how these influence their vision of life (happiness or suffering).

5. The usual break in communication between the two states symbolizes the demolition of humanity's Tower of Babel, which creates the confusion of our cosmic schizophrenia.

The resolution to our cosmic schizophrenia depends mainly on the efficient intercommunication between our dual natures.

The main problem that impairs this reconciliation is that the languages employed to communicate are incompatible. Like the brain's left hemisphere, relative nature uses reason and scientific laws, while absolute nature, like the right hemisphere, uses intuition and love as a basis for communication.

The lack of synchronization between our brain hemispheres is the origin of our cosmic schizophrenia. Relative nature is deterministic and organized. Absolute nature is spontaneous and probabilistic. The separation generated by the divergence in language between the two natures (brain hemispheres) looks a little like the one that occurred during the construction of the Tower of Babel in the old testament, which caused all the divergences of races and customs in our world.

The only possible way to restore the communication between the two is to find our original universal language. Prayer and meditation are the traditional methods promulgated by all religious philosophies to facilitate the process. The only way to coordinate this new bond is the language of love that resides in our hearts (right brain hemisphere) since our original creation.

The tricky part about this action is getting our rational side (left cerebral hemisphere, or reason) to sit at the negotiating table to bargain with our spiritual side (right cerebral hemisphere or heart).

The problem is that the rational part of the person, guided mainly by the laws of reason and science (5% of its existential reality), is afraid of losing the hegemony it has maintained for so long. **This existential conflict between the two natures is the origin of humanity's suffering throughout history.**

Like the prodigal son in the Bible, the self separates from its primary origin and home (spiritual inheritance) after asking for its material inheritance (free will, reason, temporal life). Then, the self allows its material side to guide it in a life of selfishness and individual satisfaction. This experience is enjoyable initially, but it degenerates into the natural dissatisfaction and unhappiness that time, aging, and existential loneliness create in life. Finally, the self understands that the true happiness it always searched for always existed in his father's house.

In their saddest moments, the Children of Man finally recognize their real origin, listen to their transcendental side (heart) and decide to return home. Surprisingly, the love represented by their father's forgiveness celebrates their return, for the Children of

Man return reborn as the Children of God, the Christ or Buddha who potentially live in each of us!

We are left to ask, what would have happened if the prodigal son did not experience, under his free will, the experience of creation? Wouldn't it have been easier for the father, in his wisdom and to spare his son the experience of suffering, to give him a good scolding about what would happen, thinking he would not tolerate it? Isn't that what most parents would have done?

This painful experience generates the empathy and compassion that change the Children of Man into Children of God.

Co-Creation: A Loving and Responsible Vision of the Universe

Where does our universe's perceptible (tangible) essence originate from? Does it develop regardless of our ability to perceive, based on the laws or forces of our physical world? Or do subjective individual human experiences influence it? This question encouraged the development of endless theories outlined by many philosophical schools. I'll synthesize what I got from my contact with different philosophies.

The predominant position based on established scientific laws is that everything that exists occurs regardless of human perception. Science focuses mainly on how matter and energy interrelate, where what exists is what is proven by the scientific method.

The problem with this position is that new scientific discoveries continually make many scientific laws obsolete, creating a relentless change in the previous concepts of our material world. Thus, yesterday's scientific theory becomes tomorrow's mistake.

New quantum physics, the relativity theory, the multi-dimensional strings theory, and analytical-theoretical mathematics question this deterministic scientific vision. These theories suggest that time is a relatively subjective phenomenon and that what happens in the material world is intimately affected by the observer. They also tell us that we can theorize the presence of multiple invisible dimensions additional to the three that govern our visible universe.

But, how is it that the most elementary and invisible components of the universe are grouped into increasingly complex organizations until they manifest themselves in the visible material world?

Why do the science that studies our microcosm (the world of the subatomic and invisible) and the macrocosm (the visible world) find that they seem to be timeless (no beginning or end) when the scientific laws governing its order seem to be ruled by time?

For example, there is an infinite type and amount of new subatomic particles in the microcosm that have been discovered after the "discovery" of the basic structure of the atom, which was initially defined as limited to protons, neutrons, and electrons.

Quantum physics suggests one possible theory

where the subjective influence of the observer (subject) on the elementary components of the invisible universe (object) affects how those components behave and manifest.

According to this theory, the primordial nature (antimatter?) of the universe preexists in a dormant state where all the infinite options of its possible manifestation reside and depend on how the observer organizes them in his mind.

Our understanding of the universe is like a fairy tale with no beginning or end, where the reader creates the plot as he reads. It is as if creation is instead an act of facilitation, where love is the facilitator, and the minds of humans with free will are the creators.

In this story, the plot will be full of happiness or suffering depending on the reader's free will and vision. The difference is the prevalence of the left cerebral hemisphere's exclusive (selfish) view or the inclusive (loving, supportive) vision of the right cerebral hemisphere. We could also say that it depends on the predominance of reason (cortical brain) versus love (heart, intuition). A lot is going on here!

We could visualize our known universe as a collection of concordant habits or visions, which, based on the probability that they occurred in a given space of time and the accordance of the observations of a group of individuals, become paradigms or realities acceptable to them.

The more these paradigms agree upon observation, the more accurate or genuine they seem to the spectators.

We organize the infinite potential of the primordial matrix (love) according to our subjective vision and then become attached to a specific part of it as if it were an absolute, unchangeable reality. We then transmit this vision to others without realizing our mistakes. Like people blinded by their ignorance, leading others in their path! (Fanaticism and prejudice.)

When science uses scientific methods and controls the subjectivity of observed occurrences, they call it a law.

These laws are like pictures that freeze the complex interaction of the observer and the observed during the constant creativity (love) of the primordial nature of the universe. The mind then organizes these pictures into a fictional (edited) continuity, like when a 3-hour film is edited into a 1-hour portion created by the temporal subjectivity of the brain. In that edited cut, you will lose much of the necessary experience and essence of the film.

The same is true in the development of laws that regulate the social-cultural style of different countries and races based on their group and individual experiences. Just look at the variants in what other cultures consider delicious meals, and you will see what I mean.

If we return to the three original existential questions, we would confirm that our dual nature manifests concurrently. One or the other predominates from moment to moment, depending on varied factors.

We could conclude that time is relative, that the mind of the observer artificially creates the perceptible manifestation of our visible reality (5%), and that the dissolution of this material part (death) in the relative time of what's visible does not affect the creative potential of our indiscernible nature (95%).

We also observe that the infinite matrix (love, divinity, the transcendental) and its temporal manifestation (the material universe) are in an intimate, continuously changing interrelationship.

In other words, the observer could change the universe to what he wants by merely establishing an uninterrupted, open communication with his primordial nature, guided by love in his free will. Would this be the power behind what is called "Faith"?

If this is the case, we must learn to diminish the predominance of our relative and disposable part to allow the absolute or transcendental one to participate in the creative process of the mind. Then we can change the individualism and separatism created by our selfishness. That is how we can promote the solidarity born from the bond of our spiritual family as true Children of God.

This would be the purest way to manifest love in the universe, an act of co-creation and loving co-responsibility!

The relative mind (5%), which creates the duality that separates us from our true nature, is always in an unceasing activity to sustain the apparent reality of our material universe with all the consequences of this action.

In this way, life then becomes a myriad of contrasts that the self classifies, according to its individual perception and experience, into good, bad, or neutral. Then the self promotes actions that attract the good ones, drive away the bad ones and create indifference to the neutrals.

This generates an endless cycle of pleasing emotions when we obtain good experiences and unpleasant ones when we do not receive them. As the relative presence of time brings about an inevitable change in the universe, the self cannot avoid the cycles of good experiences alongside the bad ones. There is no perfect climate, no delicacy that will not rot, no harvest without work, no metal that will not rust, no permanent personal relationship, and our bodies will age and die.

Let us all learn to make our tale one of love and solidarity, with a happy ending for all the characters!

BONUS QUESTIONS TO IMPROVE YOUR GRADE

1. How does the intention of our free will influence our role within the book or theater of life? How can we improve our influence on the plot?

2. Is free will really free?

3. Look for examples in your lives and those of others that represent our cosmic schizophrenia.

4. Imagine ways to use co-creation and co-responsibility in our lives at home, work, and in politics.

5. Review your previous concept of faith and study the one mentioned in this chapter. Why can't faith guarantee that your desires will manifest when you want them? (Suggestion: study the difference in the relative time of the Children of Man and the absolute time of the Children of God.)

6. How can I increase the chances of something I want to happen? Tip: Review the innumerable desires associated with the different beliefs of humans in their vision of the universe.

REFLECTION AND MEDITATION EXERCISE

To reduce the predominance of our relative (rational) part, we must learn to appease it. Thus, the objective of Shamata meditation is to calm our thoughts through a technique where we focus the mind in a single direction.

Although meditation techniques vary, most of them focus on sacred objects, a light (like a candle), praying repetitive phrases like the Rosary, or singing mantras. In addition, the Tibetan Buddhist tradition promotes focusing on the respiratory cycle, observing the entrance and release of air through the airways while allowing the breathing cycle to happen naturally.

You may practice counting breathing cycles (inhaling and exhaling) up to seven times. Then, when you notice your thoughts divert to something else, you must restart the sequence of seven breaths. You will be surprised by how quickly the mind deviates again. At the end of the exercise, attempt once more to locate where the Self or mind is in your body.

GOD'S NAME IS SO IMMENSE IT WON'T FIT IN MY MOUTH

Glossary - Chapter IV

Rosetta Stone— A stone found in the excavations of ancient Egyptian civilization, which yielded the key to translating their hieroglyphics.

THE EXPERIENCES THAT SEPARATE US ARE PERHAPS THE ORIGIN OF OUR RELIGIOUS DISCREPANCIES

To understand the origin of our disagreements, we must first review the factors that influence how our dual characteristics manifest and produce a subjective interpretation of our way of observing the universe.

The predominance of one of these manifestations in a person's consciousness depends on several factors:

1. The person's ability to understand the existence of these manifestations. We must realize that they exist because of scientific evidence, even if we do not perceive them with our physical senses.

2. The ability to understand their origin. (Review Chapter I.)

3. The ability to understand how they interact.

4. The ability to comprehend how they influence our contrasting visions of life (happiness or suffering).

Understanding these capabilities depends on the efficient communication between the two manifestations we physically represent as the right hemisphere (spirit-intuition-timelessness) and the left hemisphere (matter-time-reason).

76

The first two factors can be understood within the context of our temporal universe because we can infer their existence through reason and science. If you review the previous chapters, we may conclude that:

1. Our universe and bodies exist in two different ways.

2. One, governed by the laws of time and scientific knowledge, is perceptible and verifiable by our five senses and has an apparent beginning (birth) and end (death). We know it is 5% of the universe.

3. Another is inferred by the findings of quantum physics and the theory of relativity, which tells us that the remaining 95% of the universe is invisible to our five senses. It lies outside the rules of time because it has no measurable beginning or end.

We could accept that the universe, and ourselves, are made of a cosmic tapestry composed of two types of threads or filaments (antimatter and matter) but that our physical senses can only be aware of one (matter).

Suppose my previous discussion convinced you of the existence of both natures. How can we find a way to restore communication between these two? What will be the consequences of this reconnection? Remember that the alphabets of these languages are not compatible. And that we must find the Rosetta Stone that provides the translation code to remember our universal language, lost since the Tower of Babel. Perhaps then we will communicate with our imperceptible source.

Let us discuss this communicative enigma later and talk about the communication issues existing between the Children of Man in the visible universe of the five senses.

Communication Problems in the World of Matter & Time: The Battle of the Brain Hemispheres

Just as virtual barriers exist between the material and immaterial universe, some exist among the mini-universes created by our mind's individualism.

These barriers, which are limitations created by the five senses and our individual experiences and abilities, are Interference that creates discord and unhappiness between humans and between the brain hemispheres. This leads to dissenting visions of reality influenced by race, socioeconomic and geographical situations, religious views, and the educational level achieved.

It is logical and obvious that social-cultural styles and the laws ruling different nations are subjectively influenced by the previous factors. One of the most historically persistent is the difference in women's human rights within societies and religions. In addition, we already know that the varied experiences of parenting, education, and religion within the many economic and racial strata of the same country result in significant lifestyle discrepancies.

Communication issues between humans increase their connection problems with their own spiritual origin, creating infinite discrepancies in their religious views. Since my early youth, I was always intrigued by the difficulties created by the discrepant sectarian visions regarding the nature of God (the transcendent nature), which, ironically, have been the main reason for most of our wars.

Let me tell you how my interpretation of this experience helped me find the way out of this *impasse*. First, let us momentarily assume that most of us accept there is only one transcendental reality. Then, let us make a comparison to understand where so many divergences come from, even if it is a little simplistic in my representation:

Compare the transcendental nature (God-love) to a vast universal radio station that has these specific characteristics:

1. It is constantly transmitting, 24 hours a day, 7 days a week from the beginning of time.

2. Its transmission power is infinite, as it has no limits of space and time.

3. It transmits its message without interference, as it does so from the other side of the barrier, where there is no duality in manifestations of physical law.

4. The message, in its essence, is unchanging: the purest expression of love that manifests with infinite qualities, perceptible in all parts of the universe, and that brings unbiased happiness to all beings. (Compassion, wisdom, tolerance, understanding, flexibility, empathy, patience, etc.).

5. The transmission can adapt to the receptive capacity of the receiver.

Radio Receiver Interference – Where the Problem Begins

Although human beings are made in the image and likeness of God, they are limited by the inherent interference of its physical essence (the five senses and their individual experience). These limitations of the "receiving radios" are the origin of all the views of the material universe. Being limited to time and the perceptible world, the radio broadcaster (Children of God) has some limitations, which are:

1. Does not broadcast all the time.

2. It has the free will to turn on the radio and to tune in to the station of its choice or to leave it off.

3. Many of us do not turn the radio on because we are not aware of the receiver; thus, we live isolated in our physical world. Even if we turn on the radio, others only search for stations that reinforce our subjective views. We prefer what supports the isolation of our selfishness.

82

4. The limitations of the material world (the interference of our five senses, intellectual capacity, socioeconomic situation, level of education, and religious concepts) limit the quality of the reception.

Interference that promotes individuality (ego) helps create a tunnel vision of the original message.

The Name of God Is So Immense That It Does Not Fit in My Mouth

This phrase that I adapted from the Hebrew scriptures originates from their respect for the sacred name of God. From the teaching of the Kabbalah, the scriptures gave God various designations, representing the many inherent qualities of his power. However, all of them originated from the only written form that produced all the other names, YHWH, the Tetragrammaton. Which, according to Hebrew tradition, was unpronounceable and doing so was blasphemous.

Hearing this, I immediately questioned the teacher: "How can I refer to this manifestation of God, respecting the Hebrew tradition?" The teacher answered: you just must refer to Him as, "that who's name is so immensely great, that I cannot fit in my mouth." My interpretation of this phrase takes a less literal turn, since it reflects the complexity and infinity of the concept of divinity, which the self, ruled mainly by its physical senses, is not able to grasp.

Since time and the senses govern the human perception, humans can't understand the immensity of our spiritual part without first reducing it in size to fit in our mouth (mind), so we can chew and assimilate its meaning. This interpretation of the antimaterial self, no matter how clear it appears to the mind, is still tainted by the subjective influence created by our physical senses.

Humans, in their search for the original source, do not realize that they only receive a minimal and individual part of the transmission from the Great Radio

Transmitter (tubular vision). Although this vision could inspire and satisfy us with happiness, joy, and hope, it is only a very subjective part of our spiritual side and does not necessarily have to agree with that of other individuals that are also tuned in to the universal station.

These divergent views may guide humans to think that instead of man being made in the image and likeness of the creator, God is made in the image and likeness of man. We all know some people who believe this, don't we?

Rebroadcasting Will Naturally Amplify the Distortion of the Original Transmission

The Self begins to broadcast, unknowingly, a distorted transmission of the original program in its joy at sharing its fulfilling message with others. The interference created by the physical senses is amplified when others rebroadcast their own tainted perceptions, like when gossip distorts information as it spreads from one person to the next!

Those who receive the original message from their own perspective will find various discrepancies with the one heard by others, thus initiating the first religious divergences.

In their search for their origin, humans do not realize that everyone is receiving a very individualized and appropriate message and do not understand that others also hear it according to their own perspectives. Therefore, perhaps the easiest way to get to know God would be to learn from all the individual visions that humans hold, for "[...] the Kingdom of God is in your midst" (Luke 17:21).

We could then postulate that to improve our shared relationships and life experiences, we would have to improve communication from all human perspectives and among all the participants.

Communication problems will influence the human experience at several levels:

1. Humans' communication with their transcendental Self (God)

2. Humans with themselves

3. Humans with others

The quality and clarity of the communication between the last two levels will be directly proportional to that of humans with their spiritual source.

This suggests that the most appropriate way to know yourself is to recognize your internal divinity and identify how it reflects our inner universe (Self). Then, to realize that our inner source is also shared by all other beings, allowing us to acknowledge the authentic bond of our humanity, created by the common lineage of love.

The phrase "Love your neighbor as yourself" (Mathew 22:39) comes from that bond that automatically generates the golden law: "Don't do to others what you don't like them to do to you" and the obvious one: "So in everything, do to others what you would have them do to you [...]" (Mathew 7:12).

This interaction between the two natures constantly occurs since the boundless universal station is transmitting continuously. Yet, its influence depends on the free will of humans to tune in or not and which station they prefer. (Do you understand now how we self-inflict our suffering with selfishness' masochistic hand?)

We cannot then blame or hold the divinity or other humans accountable for the suffering we created with our unconscious selfish actions. Perhaps now you will understand Jesus' words on the cross, "Father, forgive them, for they do not know what they are doing." (Luke 23:34.)

Divine love is like that of a universal parent, who regards the children of creation as beings she loves equally and who allows them to learn from their experience at their own pace, without preconceived expectations. The Self deceives itself when it believes to be a favorite of the great parent of the universe.

But, how can we learn to look at the universe through the eyes of the spirit? The ability to balance our dual nature will provide us with a solution. How we will carry out the following actions will be the subject of the next chapter.

1. The ability to understand how our dual natures interact

2. The ability to know how they influence our vision of life (happiness or suffering). (This is the chapter that will look like a tragic soap opera!)

BONUS QUESTIONS TO IMPROVE YOUR GRADE

1. Is there a religion that fully communicates the nature of God (love)?

2. Why is our history full of armed conflicts related to religious beliefs?

3. How can humans improve their communication with others?

4. How can you improve your communication with God?

5. Let us look for the basis of forgiveness by reviewing the last chapters. What is the leading cause of our selfish actions?

REFLECTION AND MEDITATION EXERCISE

Repeat the exercise in the previous chapter, then take the time to carefully observe your interaction with your environment. Look at your daily routines, such as your personal grooming, dressing (Which shoe do you put on first?, Which sleeve do you put in first?) Notice your breakfast routine. Observe your respiratory cycle, and notice the difference in rate and temperature between inhalation and exhalation. Throughout your ritual, watch what your mind is doing.

Try to chew your food at least twenty times and be aware of individual tastes. Avoid controversial topics and discussions during your meals. Does your mind wander off to another place or activity? Practice keeping your mental focus on the action in your present time. Take a good look at your interaction with your colleagues at work and try to figure out how they feel: Are they sad or cheerful? Notice how you feel emotionally about each one of them. Why do you like or sympathize with some people better than others? What factors led you to reach that conclusion?

The next time you are upset about an action or comment from a colleague, ask yourself whether their intention was to annoy you or if it could have been a misinterpretation of their response. Then, after calming down, if you have an unpleasant experience with a coworker, let them know that you were affected by that action without judging or criticizing them. And then observe their response.

As you leave your home, gift a smile to everyone and watch its effect on others. Please do not do this only with the gender you are attracted to; you may have ambiguous responses! Before you lose your patience, count until you get tired or do some complex mathematical in your head. This activates the rational part of your brain and will spare you many inappropriate responses. Finally, reread all previous chapters and learn to look at the universe through the eyes of the Spirit.

WHEN HUMANS LEARNS TO LOOK AT THE UNIVERSE THROUGH THE EYES OF THE SPIRIT (HEART) THEY ONLY SEE LOVE.

Glossary - Chapter V

Interdependence— The natural condition of the universe, based on its holographic character and where all its parts are spun by the threads of Love. In this manifestation, the action or effect on one of its components reverberates across the whole universe. This represents the unity and solidarity of all creation (as in the Three Musketeers, "One for all and all for one").

THE MEETING OF OUR NATURES AT THE NEGOTIATING TABLE (THE HEART)

In the previous chapter, after establishing the existence of our two manifestations, we discussed how we could restore communication between them using a meditation technique.

In this chapter, we will focus on trying to understand how they interact, how they influence each other, how they manifest themselves in the universe, and how they impact our way of looking at life with the experience of happiness or suffering.

How can we sit these two natures at the negotiating table? How can we encourage them to communicate openly, thus promoting the individual happiness of the self and that of the universe inclusively? This would achieve a harmonious interdependence between both.

We have already discussed how the matter-time part of existence (Children of Man), led by the limitations of the five senses, created a state of individualism or selfishness where every being who lives feels independent of those that share his experience. This state functionally transforms our living experience into a mental prison, where the bars are made of the metal of time and space falsely generated by our five senses.

Remember how time creates the illusion of birth and death, giving priority to the needs of the material nature of the self, which generates the anxiety to take advantage of existing, efficiently and pleasantly, in the shortest possible amount of time? We may also feel that all beings agree in the need for individual happiness. Still, their different perspectives may lead to disagreements on how to achieve this.

The problem created by this view comes from the self's individualism and independence, promoted by its apparent free will. This results in actions that promote happiness in some but suffering in others. History is full of examples since the beginning of life on this planet, which continue with the current exploitation of man and nature.

Reestablishing Our Communication While Seated at the Negotiating Table

We already know the problem was the discrepancy of languages between our two natures, separated by the barriers of time and space, forcing us to find the key that unites both languages or a passageway between the two worlds.

Remember, it was man's mind that created the time barrier when they separated the two worlds. Then, the key to harmonize the apparent discrepancy could be to evaluate the validity of our mental process.

From the beginning of the search to decipher our origin, which brought the different religious concepts, the original channels of communication were established mainly through third parties (messengers) or by magical interpretations of natural processes.

However, the most common way to develop our inner conversation was always prayer and meditation.

The problem with prayer is that, by its own limitations, is directed to one goal, mostly the divine source, creating a unidirectional transmission. In communication systems it is usual to receive confirmation of our message by a response from the receiver.

There can be no real communication between two parties if we do not receive confirmation or a reaction to our message, and thus establish a two-way connection!

If the above is true, the solution to the conundrum of our cosmic schizophrenia is to accept the presence of our transcendental origin. Thus, we could then restore or reconnect with the creative force and sit with it at the negotiating table of our hearts.

When the Self breaks the deceptive barrier of individualism and looks through the eyes of the spirit, then it holds a broader perspective of the universe. Like when an explorer looks at the valley after climbing the highest mountain. "When the Self looks at the universe through the eyes of the Spirit, it only finds love."

In the journey through time and space, true free will comes from the power of love. This makes humans co-responsible for their actions and consequences during his voyage. In the world of matter and energy, according to Newton's laws, every effort entails a similar and proportional reaction to preserve the balance of the universe.

Therefore, every action that occurs in the universe is interdependent (affects all its parts), including those of its children. And, from these observations, we see logical empathy in the Golden Rule: "Don't do to others what you don't want them to do to you."

Let us also remember that humans can't understand their universe clearly due to interference from the five senses and their individual experiences according to upbringing, education, social level, religious vision, and race.

Those beings, by experiencing some form of interconnection with their transcendental nature (the Great Universal Radio Broadcaster), have individual interference and have a valid, albeit limited, understanding of their transcendental reality.

This realization should unite us and help us to listen, learn, and tolerate the infinite ways that humans perceive the immeasurable nature of God.

Most religious prayers are of the one-way type we mentioned earlier, like the "sound that occurs when a tree falls into a solitary forest." If we do not wait to hear the answer at the end of the prayer, it will appear to fall on deaf ears.

The purpose of meditation as the final part of prayer is to establish connectivity and tune in to the best station with less interference. There are several meditation techniques depending on personal religious beliefs. Still, they all attempt to pacify our thoughts and establish a state of mind of maximum relaxation and harmony. Modern research shows that the meditative state alters brain waves as well as multiple aspects of human physiology.

Therefore, the key to escaping our mind's prison is to pacify our mental activity through meditation. Meditation becomes the Rosetta Stone, which allows us to openly interconnect our two natures (brain hemispheres) under one universal language: love.

Visualize that the virtual barrier dividing our two realms is the continuous chatter of the mind (Ego) in its relentless effort to maintain the sandcastles that the sea of time destroys repeatedly.

To find the gaps in this barrier, we have to lower the energy that creates it, which is thought, until it stops for a few moments, allowing us to find passageways that give us a glimpse of what is on the other side.

The great Masters of all religious philosophies managed, in their meditative states, to destroy the imaginary barrier by creating a harmonious union of the two worlds.

These great beings learned to look at the universe and humans with the eyes of the spirit, reflecting love over all creation.

We could conclude that the interaction between our two natures is such that the transcendental, which exists outside of time, create the material side that time can influence. But the self and its individuality (ego) are not aware of its exact origin. Thus initiating an apparent disconnect between the two manifestations described previously as cosmic schizophrenia, originated in time by the experience of birth, aging, and dying, promoting individualism and selfishness. This eventually leads to the unceasing contrasts of joy and suffering in life (the prison created by the five senses).

After humans recognize their origin, sit at the negotiating table (heart), and wield the key to free themselves from the prison they created with their minds, they find themselves looking at each other with the eyes of the Spirit and find only love in creation. As I said in my poem at the beginning, *"This new vision, born of our own heart and all the beings of this Universe, dissolves all vestige of suffering away from our being when we understand that happiness has always been with us on this path without beginning or end."*

BONUS QUESTIONS TO IMPROVE YOUR GRADE

1. Look within yourself for examples of the different types of interference that interrupted the communication between our two mental states.

2. Explain the differences in the types of communication used in prayer and meditation.

3. Explain how cosmic schizophrenia can lead to depression, anxiety, and anger. Identify the precipitating factors in your life that promote these conditions.

4. Take an in-depth look at the concept of life as a prison created by our own minds. Study your preferences, habits, and social styles and see which ones help or hinder you to live in solidarity, with harmony and peace.

5. How can the assumption that we can make mistakes when interpreting our exchanges with others help us live happier lives?

REFLECTION AND MEDITATION EXERCISE

After reviewing our previous practices, today we will use our imagination and visualization. These are other ways to focus the mind, like breathing, which also have beneficial subliminal effects on our mental state. Depending on our personal beliefs about divinity, we can use religious images or symbols. For example, a Christian may use Christian statues, a practitioner of Eastern philosophies will use his own, and one who sees divinity more impersonally will do so with symbols of light, color, or geometric designs.

After calming the mind through breathing exercises, use your thoughts to project a beautiful shower of love that will bathe you in all the colors of the rainbow.

A COLORFUL BATH OF LOVE

Sitting in a comfortable position with your back straight and head upright, visualize a source of spiritual strength or energy that makes you feel protected. For example, the figure of the Sacred Heart of Jesus, of youthful appearance, smiling and standing, with his arms open and emanating rays of multicolored light from the center of his heart to yours, where there is a small seed.

Understand the meaning of the exercise. Jesus represents the human manifestation of the Holy Spirit, which is the force of love left to us by God after his son left. The multicolored rays represent the infinite ways in which love could manifest itself among humans. The seed in your heart represents the possible way in which love resides in humans.

As these rays of light begin to fill your heart, feel loved and protected by the love of God, and watch as the little seed begins to open and, in turn, emanates the multiple colors of love everywhere. Imagine how those colors bathe you in love and reach all parts of our bodies, especially those where there is some discomfort or disease, and visualize how these aches and pains are pacified and healed.

After you feel fulfilled with joy and wellness, in gratefulness, share this meditation with all human beings, especially those who have hurt us in the past in their ignorance for not feeling loved.

Visualize multicolored rays that reflect from your heart towards all human beings, without distinction, including those who have left this world and those who, in your way of thinking, have brought suffering into your live. Dedicate a few minutes to this action and then rest your mind in silence for a few extra minutes. End the meditation giving thanks for this opportunity. Do this exercise every day when you get up and when you go to bed.

In the end, to keep your mind in a state of tranquility, imagine that your thoughts are like clouds in the sky and that your state of mind is like the stillness of the blue color of heaven. Let your thoughts pass as if they were clouds, without following them, and focus on the blueness of the sky, your natural state.

THE MELODIOUS SILENCE OF THE COSMOS

*Silence yearns to quench the Soul's unending thirst for
Love, yet in its splendor, it fails to muffle the
continuous yet fleeting chatter of the ego, for the Soul
has long forgotten its majestic tranquility.
How will I be able, then, to arouse the remembrance
of its melodious song again?*

*I have already realized that this will not occur by
increasing the volume of the dissonant notes of my
mundane life.
Nor by recalling all the memories of my frivolous
experiences, which only ignite more the flames of my
insatiable desire for them.
Nor by reigniting the infernal passions that muted,
even more, my sense of hearing.*

*How can I then stifle the deafening shame of the
condemning voices that punish my heart?
Perhaps only by realizing that all my lapses were
committed with the innocence of intention and
stipulated by the ignorance of my divine linage.*

108

Clearly established by our great Teacher, Jesus, who in his last words said, "Father, forgive them, for they do not know what they are doing."

My heart then finally finds peace, as I understand that in the forgiveness of my transgressions, and those done to me by others, resides the final solution to my paradox.
And then, suddenly, a thunderous emptiness permeates every corner of my Universe, reawakening in my heart the Melodious Silence of the Cosmos.

THE PARALLEL WORLDS CREATED BY OUR MIND

THE SPIRITUALLY-BLIND NEVER FIND LOVE

When we apply the golden rule to communication among humans, we allow love to guide our minds.

We have already mentioned in other chapters how each individual's experience creates infinite views of the world according to genetics, cultural background and the habits or customs that result from it. We also talked about how these perceptions cause concordance or discrepancy in our living experience, established to govern our lives in harmony or discord. We should remember that "The pursuit of happiness is one of the few actions in which human beings agree, even if they disagree on what it means and how to find

111

it" (Chapter II). Ironically, much of humanity's suffering arises from this discrepancy in the pursuit of happiness.

We could then affirm that out of the infinite, individual and divergent ways of looking at life, humans creates parallel mental worlds. These worlds increasingly isolate them into their already existing emptiness or existential loneliness. That is why I mention in my poem that solitude *"... still exists within the clamorous effervescence of crowds."* And in the previous chapter, I said, "This state functionally transforms our living experience into a mental prison, where the bars are made of the metal of time and space falsely generated by our five senses."

In the past, the gathering of individuals in groups that later united in more complex social organizations led to the development of civilized nations that nurtured our history. Without going into the complex role of individuals within socio-economic structures or the political systems that have governed them, I would like to limit this discussion to the close interrelationship of the individual with others within his social environment, such as their role in family, work, and religious activities.

Concerning our daily exchanges, persons do not realize, paradoxically, that what they think, what they say and what they mean do not always agree. Another incongruity exists between what they believe, what they hear, what others say, and the interpretation of what they heard. Proverbs 10:19 expressed it more elegantly by saying, "Sin is not ended by multiplying words, but the prudent hold their tongues."

If this is reality, what can we be sure of in our interpretation of what we observe? It should also be noted that the messages of our nonverbal communication are also part of our exchange. Science assures us that only 7% of our interpretations are based on the words we hear, 13% is based on voice, expression, intonation, etc., and 80% on body language. That is why I jokingly say that to stop the relentless talk of a Latino, we just have to tie his hands!

What can we do to improve our communication skills? The goal is to eliminate all interference generated by our individual bias. Later in the book there are meditation techniques to reduce these interferences.

The first thing we can do is establish a two-way conversation with our transcendent reality (God, spirit etc.) using:

1. Prayer- Conversation directed from us to God.

2. Meditation- Listening to God's answer (some people never have time or are too busy to listen).

This bidirectional connection with divinity gradually changes the way we look at the world, seeing it through the eyes of the Spirit, thus eliminating all the interference selfishness creates using the five senses.

Let us look at some common impediments to good communication during our daily exchanges.

The Spiritually Blind Are the Difficult People in Our Lives: The Un-loved, Those Who Jesus Referred to as Those That Do Not Know What They Do

Although difficult people manifest themselves in numerous ways, they all have a common denominator: dreadful self-esteem, with little tolerance for criticism and minimal insight of how their actions affect others.

These are the selfish ones, who, as spiritually-lame beings, use others as crutches to walk the path of life. They are also the spiritually-blind who can never find love, for they do not love or let themselves be loved.

These are those who were not nurtured during their upbringing and, therefore, never learned what love is! I call them the "unloved ones". Sayings like, "I call it how I see it," "That's in my genes," "Take it or leave it," are some of the phrases we often hear from them.

Lack of self-esteem situates them in a defensive posture and in a state of constant alert. Since they don't like anything within themselves, they live in constant criticism of what they see around them and the people with which they relate.

Lack of self-awareness makes them intolerant, perfectionists and demanding to such a degree that they are never satisfied with their actions or those of others. These "difficult ones" like to stay on the offensive mode, using criticism, verbal aggression, and sarcasm to intimidate others.

We could sum up that the difficult ones like to live in forts walled off by their ignorance of their transcendental reality, which does not let them enjoy the power of love they forgot they had and now do not recognize. This ignorance leads them to fear, frustration, and anger when they cannot control the world around them.

How do we deal with these people?

First, know that they have no power over you, except for what you allow them to have. Second, they are fragile persons with abysmal self-esteem who do not feel loved or know how to love.

That is why they attack preemptively: to hide their weakness because they feel they are worthless and want to bring you down to their level (they use the same preventive tactic of many powerful nations!).

If they persist in their actions despite your efforts to love them, you should know the act that affects them the most is to ignore or disregard them. So keep going your way and leave them alone playing within their own fecal waste (my editor did not like the synonym I used here!)

The difficult ones' behavioral patterns (unloved ones) often originate from their family and personal experience's programming. Many powerful suggestive messages come from these influences, which subliminally become part of our personalities.

Let me give you an example from my own upbringing.

For many years, I was told I was very clumsy, as I had a tendency to break my toys and it became difficult for me to learn how to tie my shoes (they didn't know it was an excellent excuse to make them tie them for me!). At the midpoint through my medical education, I was very attracted to the surgical fields, but was hesitant to take this road because of my "clumsy" reputation. This had a happy ending when, rotating through the psychiatrist clinics, my group was practicing visual-manual coordination exercises used to measure maturing manual skills in children.

To my surprise, I was the fastest to carry them out. I still remember the psychologist's words: "Mr. Figueroa, have you considered dedicating yourself to surgery, since your skills are above average?" This was sufficient to question my groundless fears and to embark on a very successful career in the field of pediatric surgery. Could this person be an angel or a messenger of love in my life?

Continuing our discussion about the problematic or difficult people, I contend that their ignorance of their own potential leads them to frustration, fear, and anger when they cannot control the world around them. They, like the many who condemned Jesus to die on the cross, were the spiritually-blind who could not understand the message of love. This reality produced the most loving message from Jesus in the Bible, one that you have seen repeatedly in this book.

"Father, forgive them because they do not know what they are doing." (Luke 23:43). Since Jesus was looking at them through the eyes of the spirit, he recognized the spiritual bond that, as brothers and sisters in the Spirit, made them brethren of Jesus and children of God.

The great sages of many Eastern spiritual traditions taught their disciples that these difficult beings sometimes became our best teachers, as they could test our ability to love, tolerate, and forgive in the most trying circumstances.

Sometimes our life's challenges are stimulating events that promote our success. Let me give you a personal example. Although I was always an outstanding student in my high school years, I was never known for my admirable behavior.

In my 3rd-year chemistry class, I was unlucky enough to be in a group of three equally unruly males, which gained our teacher's enmity. This negatively influenced the grading of our scholastic performance and led me to have, for the first time ever, a "C" in a class.

In the middle of the last semester, we were offered a national chemistry aptitude test in which I broke the curve in the downward direction. To top it all off, the teacher, when giving me the grade in front of the whole class, said, "Mr. Figueroa, I don't know what you're going to study, but I recommend you not pursue anything to do with the sciences." Can you imagine how I felt? Interestingly, I accepted it as a challenge to prove her wrong. From that moment on, I got "A's" in all my exams, and I ended up with an average of "B+" in the course (although I think I deserved an "A"!).

Surprisingly, during my participation in a summer science camp the same year at a local university, I re-took the same test I had failed in high school and, as it turned out, I got the highest grade of the group. And to finish the story, my grade average in the chemistry courses in my premedical curriculum was an "A".

Returning to the un-loved ones, it is not easy to deal with these troublesome individuals unless our self-esteem is well strengthened by the clarity of our communication with our transcendent source (so that we are full of love). If we are not connected, we will feel threatened by all the trick-or-treat techniques they use to intimidate us.

We all have a certain degree of "difficulty" (ask your partners if you do not believe me!) that tend to manifest during situations of tremendous emotional pressure. We usually keep it under control in our daily routines. However, the fearful or spoiled child we all have inside quickly emerges in difficult situations.

And until meditation manages·to influence the way we look at life, what mechanisms can we use to improve our communication in the short term?

The Short-Term Action Plan

The first thing is to be aware of our mental status when starting an exchange (mindfulness). Do we initiate it in a state of fear, courage, or selfishness from either side?

It is essential to know that negative emotional patterns increase the communication's interference by creating a static noise that deafens transmission. That is why it is crucial to postpone dialogue until these feelings are appeased. This state of alertness or awareness is one of the goals of meditation.

Second, we must be aware of our subjectivity and the infinite ways in which we can interpret our world. The phrase "know thyself first," which originated with ancient Delphic Greek philosophy written at the temple of Apollo, should set the tone for our communicative action. What were our previous experiences and our opinions of the person involved? How has our experience during childhood influenced us when facing similar situations? (These usually remain as obsolete programs in our psychological software.)

If we have had negative experiences with a person in the past, our reaction may already be tainted without basis. What are our personality's weaknesses of that could over-sensitize us in some instances? For example, the person could remind us of an authoritarian figure of our past. We could react to this memory and not to the action of the present individual. This is how many of our spontaneous activities are instinctively programmed.

Humans, like other animals, (although sometimes not accepted as such) can be trained to respond to many situations automatically, without being in conscious control of their actions. That is why most advertising and marketing techniques use subliminal suggestions to promote the consumption of their products.

Our life's experiences continually show us that our initial impression, good or bad, of many persons can change significantly when we get to know them better. If this is true, we must avoid the natural tendency to prejudge our interpretation of the actions of those with whom we have already had negative experiences.

The best way to deal with difficult people is to avoid projecting ourselves as a threat to them, such as when we make them aware of their mistakes or return the same aggressive tones in our communication.

"Do not corner the cat that resides in each being, or face the consequences," "Do not feed the fire with your emotional breeze." The only thing we manage by

124

bringing out their dirty laundry is an immediate or delayed defensive/aggressive reaction, which in turn generates suffering for everyone involved.

We must remember that these difficult men and women respond to flattery, patience, rational communication of how their actions affect others, and clarifying questions that help resolve the conflict. But, if we are not ready to seek the gold medal of patience in the Olympic competition against the difficult ones, sometimes it is better to avoid them and continue our training with meditation! (Remember not to allow bullying since it will promote their strength.)

Open-Bidirectional Communication

Open communication involves:

1. Visual and body awareness- Your eyes and body should be focused to the one who is addressing you. Do not scatter around when you talk.

2. Body gestures should reflect openness - avoid crossed arms and legs. Keep a reasonable distance that does not intimidate the person, especially when discussions are heated, or a pandemic is present!

3. Do not become biased by your own prejudices - You must avoid analyzing, prosecuting, or modifying the content of what you hear, which means that you must learn to listen openly. Any clarifying questions should be made at the end of the other person's communication. Before you challenge a point or criticize a position, ask clarifying questions about what you perceived (which may be totally contrary to what the other meant). These questions may be like: "I thought you meant _____. Is this impression correct?" "I interpret that your position is for or against _____, am I right?"

4. If you feel emotionally affected by the expression, be patient and think about the possibility that the other's intention was not what you think, and *you might be wrong in your interpretation.*

5. Remember that we only use 5% of the universal data! (Check the first chapter.) If you feel emotions influencing your communication skills, wait for your turn and clarify that you have been emotionally affected by your interpretation, and allow the person to clarify their intent.

6. Always use clear terms to express how you feel about their communication and never pre-judge the initiator as responsible for what you understood using words such as rude, insensitive, liar, sexist, offensive, etc. These terms close the channels of communication to the rational and objective flow they should have.

7. Look through the eyes of the Spirit - When the other party is losing control emotionally, look at it as when a child has a tantrum. Do not respond at their level and use a low and cordial tone of voice, cease the intervention, excuse yourself and suggest postponing the discussion to a later time.

8. If any comment made you feel offended, do not leave it repressed in the subconscious part of your

mind, as you are only hurting yourself. Since **"Anger is the poison we prepare for the one who offends us, but we are the ones who drink it"** (unknown author). After the other person calms down, communicate how you felt without judging and allow them to clarify their communication. When the conversation is completely broken, a possible solution is a private written note, letting the person know their position and how this breach of communication affects both parties. If the person is a loved one, reinforce the love and importance they have in your life.

9. Do not corner the cat that resides in every person, unless you want to feel like a dog that flees with his tail between his legs! "Let any one of you who is without sin be the first to throw a stone at her." (John 8:7). Remember how you felt when you made mistakes that were publicly elucidated. If you practice what this phrase suggests, your friends' list will be immeasurable! This is one of the most effective ways to practice tolerance and forgiveness. No one likes to have their mistakes made public. The phrase "I forget,

but will not forgive," is one of the main reasons for the dissolution of friendships and marriages in the world. These emotional scars that remain in the memory of the supposedly affected hinder the open communication that existed in the relationship, where love no longer flows openly.

10. The phrase "don't rub it in" is another way of promoting the attitude of not forgetting. Another equivalent is "I told you so." (Do you remember someone who used it frequently?) Some other threatening and familiar phrases that create this sense of cornering are: "As I expected", "How many times do I have to tell you?" "What more could you expect from him/her?", etc. That is why we do not do to others what we do not want them to do to us (the Golden Rule) and do not corner the cats of our lives. Remember the Beatles song, "Let it be, let it be."

BONUS QUESTIONS TO IMPROVE YOUR GRADE

1. How can we eliminate the feeling of existential loneliness from our lives?

2. Identify the problematic or difficult people (spiritually-lame) that use you as a crutch in their lives. Identify the ones you use as crutch in your journey.

3. Study and implement the five qualities of open communication. Keep track of your results.

4. Give examples of how we can learn to "look with the eyes of the Spirit." (Suggestion: look at every person as if they were family: mother, father, children, and siblings)

5. Remember moments when you were cornered by others. Remember when you cornered others. How did you feel in every situation? Save your answers for the final exam review.

REFLECTION AND MEDITATION EXERCISE

Review your life and the mistakes you made. Remember those you hurt one way or another. Review the events that culminated in those wounds. Do not forget who supported you in those moments and how you felt when they did. Look at how difficult it is to remember the sad events of your life. What feelings show up when you do? Can you really erase them from your memory? Did you really have absolute control, knowledge, and the maturity to avoid them at the time they occurred? Were you solely responsible for the situation? Do an act of repentance of events without assigning guilt. Learn from the experience, so you do not repeat it.

Repeat the visualized meditation in the previous chapter, and when viewing the rainbow bath, focus on where the feelings of guilt are located, and wipe out these spots with the colors of love and forgiveness. In the end, visualize that from the center of your heart infinite multicolored rays emanate in all directions of the universe and reach the hearts of all that you have reviled. Notice how, in doing so, they smile back to you with joyfulness. Finally, meditate in silence.

TAKING RESPONSIBILITY FOR OUR LIVES AS CO-CREATORS OF OUR UNIVERSES

Glossary - Chapter VII

Codependence - A psycho-social relationship considered inappropriate due to lack of maturity of how the parties behave. It is addictive and self-destructive for all parties, creating suffering for all. A dominant (perpetrator-codependent) party and a subjected one (victim-dependent) establish a relationship where both create a need (addictive conduct) with the other. The victim feels that they cannot survive without the abusive person, and the dominant believes that only they can fulfill the victim's needs. The common denominator to both is the lack of self-esteem and attention deficit (love) that can only be satisfied

133

externally. Many sexual abuse relationships happen because of these situations. Now you know where all those romantic songs that say they will not live without their beloved come from.

Uncertainty Principle - The principle of quantum physics established by Dr. Heisenberg, who found that the observation method affected the results in experiments studying subatomic particles. For the first time in science, he suggested that the observer could change the outcome of an experiment. In simpler words, the observer's vision changes according to the color of the lens with which the observer looks at the universe at that moment or "Beauty is in the eye of the beholder."

Rational Mind - The left-brain hemisphere, world of space and time, son of humans.

Transcendental Mind -The right-brain hemisphere, son of God.

134

<u>Spiritually-lame</u> - The dominant person in codependent relationships, who uses the dependent one as a crutch to walk the path of their life.

THE FINAL RECONCILIATION BETWEEN THE RATIONAL MIND AND THE TRANSCENDENTAL MIND

When we transform the Creator's (God) codependent relationship with his Creation (humans) to one of interdependence and solidarity, it brings the rebirth of a new person within us.

The material discussed in Chapters V and VI emphasizes the confusion caused by:

1. The lack of communication between all our dual characteristics: reasoning-love, knowledge-wisdom, science-spirituality, and rationality-intuition.

2. The tendency to look at the universe exclusively with the rational side of our minds. That

unconsciously leads us to conclude that we exist independently from others and the universe we share. Also, that the rules that govern that relationship are pre-established by immutable laws of science.

This rational view of the world creates an unceasing concern for understanding what can happen in its immediate future, leading humans to accept its lack of permanence and fragility. This can make life a process of survival of the most skilled and powerful, much like the animal kingdom's evolutionary law.

This experience leads humans to accept the reality of disease, aging, and death as inevitable circumstances. And that, in turn, will direct the Self to try to slow the progression of these situations any way they can. (Perhaps this caused the discovery of the New World, with Ponce de León seeking the fountain of youth, and the successful emergence of plastic surgery.)

When the Self realizes the unpredictability of time and quality of life, they need to pursue actions that assure them individual happiness at all costs, without considering how they could impact everything around them (selfishness). But, unfortunately, this individuality leads them to confuse the satisfaction of having achieved their goals with the real feeling of happiness when we feel loved.

Instead of achieving respect for their own worth, they prefer to be feared and use that fear to fulfill their subjective needs.

According to the ego, success depends only on individual effort. It does not recognize the importance of the efforts of others in its accomplishments, nor does it sympathize with those who cannot emulate its actions. Therefore, the person will never allow themselves to be loved, for this action would imply they need someone to love them. They think they live within an imaginary protective firewall, where only some persons can pass with the secret password, limited to the few who nurture their selfish needs.

These people thrive off recognition and flattery because they are like **energetic vampires** (spiritually-lame) who wither slowly without that external source of energy.

The extreme individualism, reinforced by their upbringing and the genetic programming, becomes the ego or individual personalities from which selfishness originates.

Selfishness, the Main Reason for Humanity's Suffering

Selfish people never achieve the satisfaction of feeling truly loved. Living, if we do so with selfishness and lack of awareness of our interdependence with the laws of the universe and other beings, becomes a nightmare of suffering with brief moments of happiness.

The search for the way out of this intolerable situation often leads to a nihilistic view of life, where individualism and selfishness reign. In the past, this motivated some wise masters to interpret the answer to the questions, "Who am I? Where do I come from? Where am I going to?" according to their unique historical, social, and geographical situations, defining the countless religious concepts that govern us today.

These great sages, who guided humans in their first steps in the process of civilization and social interaction, developed these philosophies, so necessary for proper coexistence. Unfortunately, however, they offered humans this information very selectively, assimilated according to their understanding in limited portions. To comprehend this, review the contents of chapter IV.

The problem with sectarianism and religious proselytism that still affects humanity was the intolerance that promoted wars and social oppression when nations attempted to impose one religion over the previous traditional beliefs.

The Self's Codependent Relationship with God

Because of communication errors between the individual interpretation of the Creator (God) and the individual interference of his creation (humans), and promoted by the hierarchical structures of all religions that now exist, people developed a type of codependent relationship with the "divinity" that, in many cases, paradoxically, did not alleviate the suffering of the human race.

These codependent relationships are characterized by a dependence on another person or belief to feel happy that completes their apparent deficiencies and has addictive characteristics.

This was the origin of many religious beliefs throughout history!

Codependent People's Characteristics
Low self-esteem
Repressed, insensitive
Obsessive-compulsive
Manipulative, controlling
Unrealistic
Dependent
Insecure
Lack of initiative

The misinterpretation of this codependent relationship can lead humans to a sense of guilt and confusion, to interpret the world as a "valley of tears" in which their roles are to accept that of being victims of the experience of suffering as a deserved inevitable result. Thus, their only option is to hand over all their autonomy and decision-making (free will) to the

Creator (God) and to the religious structure that guarantees them "salvation" for their souls and removal from their valley of tears.

The religious system originating from this relationship offers indulgences if specific rules of life are obeyed and certain punishments if broken. Although this relationship does not exist in every situation, there will always be a connection of the Self with "their God" that will result in various degrees of codependency.

The result is religious skepticism. Although courageous in their questioning based on scientific materialism, Atheists become alienated from any metaphysical process. Nevertheless, it must be admired that they still manage to establish ethical relationships and respect for their humanity.

Healing the Codependent Relationship by Creating One of Interdependence

The way out from fanatical codependence relationships relies on the people's understanding of how their relationship with their Creator is one of shared responsibilities (co-responsibility).

In other words, there is an interdependent relationship between the Creator and his creation. As previously explained, science supports this belief, stating that we are three-dimensional manifestations in time and space (matter) that originate from our transcendental nature of non-linear time or space (antimatter).

To understand this, you should review Chapter I, where we explained that the universe is divided into 95% timeless imperceptible antimatter and 5% perceptible temporal universe matter, where life's subjective experience depends on the intentional vision and action created by our free will.

Also, we must remember our true origin and understand that the experience of life is only one, where the transcendental manifests itself in an infinite and changing range of possibilities, and where its opposites interdependence (matter-antimatter, Children of God-Children of Man, relative mind-absolute mind, left cerebral hemisphere-right brain hemisphere, etc.) is inevitable.

Our left brain hemisphere (relative material mind) or Ego fills us with fear and reinforces our vision of codependence, generating our state of individuality. That encourages us to forget that the origin of all this suffering is the ignorance of our true transcendental origin or absolute nature. This hemisphere reinforces our belief that we are only what is born and dies, which originated from our ancestor's DNA.

This egotistical mind (rational mind) is also responsible for the tendency to project human qualities to the creative force of the universe, where **the self, which should have been made in the image and** likeness of God, distorts the image of his Creator by defining it according to its own human limitations. This trend repeats itself in almost every description of God found in many of the sacred books of all Western and Eastern civilizations.

Our right hemisphere (transcendental mind) supports us in recognizing our infinite potential when we understand our true nature and origin and the importance of our free will. This gives us a choice to live interdependently with others, like how musical notes blend within the boundless universal symphony of love, where no single note is more important than any other. Ponder this sentence for a while!

This sense of interdependence allows us to consciously share our role in that universe and our responsibility in its co-creation. The right hemisphere or spiritual mind makes us feel that we are part of "something" before we were born and that we shall return to that something when we die. It makes us feel eternal and part of a broader evolutionary process beyond our limited earthly experience of living in time and space.

The Universe's Co-creation Originates from the Interdependent Relationship of the Transcendental (God, Love) and its Creation (Universe and Humans)

In the Chinese Taoist tradition, the universe was divided into the Yang (the sky-male) and the Yin (the earth-female), where humans were a balanced manifestation of both that stood between Heaven and Earth. My interpretation of some verses from the sacred books in the Christian tradition similarly suggests that, although the Kingdom of God was not of this world, it exists in the hearts of all humans.

This interpretation is based on Luke 17:20-21, "[…] nor will people say, 'Here it is,' or 'There it is,' because the kingdom of God is in your midst." And also, in the quotation from John 18:36, "Jesus said, 'My kingdom is not of this world. If it were, my servants would fight

146

to prevent my arrest by the Jewish leaders. But now my kingdom is from another place." So perhaps I could speculate that it was instead a matter of recognizing that regal quality within each of us, and then being able to recognize it in all our brethren: "The Christ or wise one is the one who, while living with its feet on earth, always keeps its sight on the Heavens," (my quote).

The Tremendous Responsibility of Sharing God's Co-creative Role in the Universe.

We already know there is no limit to the possible ways for the state of transcendence to manifest since it is as diverse as the number of observers.

Divinity is a facilitating (loving), non-controlling characteristic of creation that depends on the creative intention of human's free will and its manifestation within our reality of time and space (material universe).

That would lead us to conclude that the realm of the Spirit is a virtual state with infinite probabilities, and the material realm is one of alternate realities co-created by the human mind, according to scientific laws.

Is love not the universe creation's great facilitator, where if the facilitator is selfish, it generates hell, and if it is a loving person, it brings paradise?

Therefore, actions based on selfishness are born from a lack of recognition of our true origin (love) that potentially resides in every Children of Man (self), even if they have not recognized it yet. This lack of awareness makes us spiritually blind or lame and creates the need to use others as crutches, producing addictive co-dependencies to seek happiness.

The universe in the three dimensions of time, space, and distance is governed by scientific laws. One of the most important is Newton's Third Law of the Principle of Action. It describes that if a body "A" exerts an action on another body "B," "B" performs another action of equal intensity and in the opposite direction on "A" (**For every action, there is an equal and opposite reaction**). That implies that every effort in our world generates a proportional response, or every cause generates a proportionate effect.

If we review everything said so far, it follows that everything that exists, measurable and visible, is manifested by a creative mental action that originates from the infinite potential state of the Creator (love). The manifestation will depend on the intention or free will of the individual.

Suppose the self identifies as transient, individual, and independent of all that surrounds them. In that case, they will follow the painful path of suffering and the fruitless and incessant pursuit of material happiness. But, if the self recognizes their true lineage as children of the Spirit, they understand the phrase: "When humans learn to look at the universe through the eyes of Spirit, they only see love" (my quote).

Remember that the universe, in its densest manifestation in time and space, is composed of identical subatomic energy particles grouped into elemental families in the periodic table, differing from each other only in number and arrangement. It is these tenuous configuration changes that manifest the final and dramatic external differences between lead and gold!

Aren't these variations in the elements the influence of the Uncertainty Principle of Quantum Physics that postulates that all visible matter and events are influenced by the subjective mental act of the observer? Then we would have to accept that the mind is the one that organizes and classifies this universe of infinite probabilities into those that will be related to the subjective experience of the observer. We could speculate that our biological DNA (Children of Man) is programmed with our five senses to understand this universe as part of time and space.

This would be the extension of Einstein's law of the relativity of time to everything that exists in the space that defines time. It would then imply that, if time is a relative phenomenon, any manifestation within time should also be relative.

From this realization, we could conclude that every experience where we see and understand our individual mini universes (mental co-creations) will be relative and subjective to our genetic software or inheritance, to the programming we learned in our unique experiences of interacting with the physical world, and to the creation of habits and values we incorporate from our shared experience with other beings.

In this fashion, the self becomes a social and psychological entity (personality) that differentiates them according to the geographical, economic, racial, and religious environment in which they develop. Always remember that, even if we all agree on the pursuit of happiness, we will never be able to agree on

Iván Figueroa-Otero, MD

how we will find it. That is why we should be cautious with our thoughts by remembering what this anonymous philosopher said (words misattributed to the Buddha):

The thought manifests as the word;
The word manifests as the deed;
The deed develops into habit;
And habit hardens into character.
So watch the thought and its ways with care,
And let it spring from love
Born out of concern for all beings.

We could add, "not from selfishness, but from the unawareness of the love that resides in you."

From all of the above, we must understand how important is the way I judge what surrounds me since it will make me co-responsible for what I have created with my thoughts. Learn to look at the universe through the eyes of love (Spirit) and not from the selfishness that generates our suffering.

The Ego, The One Who Steals the Happiness from Our Hearts

Those who live the earthly experience are like the prince abducted in his childhood in a war, only surviving his captivity with the hope of regaining the state of abundance that he stored in his heart.

Even when he is released sometime later, no material reward will fill the emptiness in his heart. However, when someone who knows where he came from and remembers what used to be his beautiful surroundings helps him remember his true lineage and origin, he will undertake the search for his lost Kingdom again.

In this story, the kidnapper represents our Ego created by our material mind where, together with our fear and ignorance, it imprisons us in the hermetic prison of time and space where we were born. That is where we alternate fleeting times of joy and suffering with the inevitable reality of birth, aging, and death.

When the Children of Man let themselves be loved by those who recognize their true lineage (Children of God), they begin to remember their homeland and find out who they really are, where they come from, and where they are headed.

That is why the way to bring out the greatness of humans is to love them intensely without preconceived expectations. If you learn and apply this lesson, it guarantees your passing of the final test of the school of life!

Love Always Offers a Special Bargain of an Enlarged Combo of Forgiveness with Our Wrongful Actions (Sins).

Remember that the spiritual state of non-time (love) in the universe exists in a virtual form without preconceived characteristics. According to his mental intention, the self generates a corresponding state of happiness (paradise) or unhappiness (hell). Selfish actions are born from ignorance of the true nature of the self, and evil results from ignorance of the existence of good.

According to the Newtonian law of correspondence, this implies that every loving or selfish action generates a similar and proportional response to the person who initiates it and the one who perceives it. This occurs only in experiences within time and space, without affecting the spiritual world of non-time and antimatter.

This realization implies a theological conflict within the Judeo-Christian tradition since, in my perspective, it would be impossible to transgress against the transcendent nature of God (remember that God is pure love and does not understand the emotions that make us suffer. Thus, our selfish actions would only affect our brethren in our human experience—the children of Man. This would mean that, if we were to ask forgiveness, it would be to the ones who we made suffer: the children of Man.

The most loving act of the universal matrix (God-love) was to give the self free will to use reason in balance with the heart. That would allow him to live in interdependence and solidarity with his brethren according to the golden law that says, "Don't do to others what you wouldn't want them to do to you."

So, where does Divine Justice exist if no one judges the consequences of our actions? By sharing the experience in the time and space of our universe, all of our thoughts and actions, conscious or unconscious, generate corresponding reactions under Newton's law of Action and Reaction (cause and effect), which have consequences.

This is what Eastern traditions, which believe in the experience of reincarnation, call individual and group Karma. I prefer to call it the Law of Love because it allows the universe, co-created by God's children, to correct the mistakes made by them without individual punitive connotations! According to the school of our life, these are only love lessons to learn from our mistakes.

Just as the universe saves every action in the spiritual realm in its memory, so are the individual efforts recorded by the beings that inhabit it. Thus, we could speculate that, just as DNA records the history of the biological experience of the organism and influences its genetic continuity, there must be a spiritual DNA that archives the memories of the transcendental history of the self.

This cause-and-effect relationship between each mental or physical activity and its result does not involve any process of self-incrimination, independent of the experience learned in and of itself. The only thing that corrects this process is the search for balance (love) in the total individual experience of the Ego.

We could compare selfish actions to the act of "sinning," unconscious or conscious. This act generates suffering, but it never affects the love-generating matrix of the universe (God). **Therefore,**

humans "sin" against God's children, but not against God.

The results of mental or physical actions originated from the use of our free will should be pictured as the most compassionate form of love, allowing each individual a way to redeem their actions, allowing them to learn from the consequences.

That is why I said that every "sin" comes a "combo" with the option of forgiveness to redeem them.

For those who follow the Judeo-Christian and Muslim traditions that see the earthly experience as a single opportunity for the soul, the results of human actions will be decided in a final judgment where the "souls" of some who have followed the law of each tradition faithfully will be compensated by an "eternal" experience of joy in heaven. But, on the other hand, those that break the law will have "eternal" suffering in hell.

For those who feel an affinity to the concept of reincarnation, the impersonal law of cause and effect (Karma) results in repeated experiences of life which, according to their previous actions, will result in several degrees of joy or suffering. That could represent the feeling of living in heaven or hell.

What more hellish experiences than what humans have done and still do to their brethren on earth? Where is the divine justice in all the wars that have been justified while imposing religious beliefs on other people's faiths?

But even those who believe in the concept of reincarnation are not entirely correct. As I said before, we must remember our true origin and understand that the experience of life is only one, where the transcendental is manifested in an infinite and changing range of possibilities. God, as the source of all souls, is living the human experience in each of its children as musical notes in the symphony of its love. The interdependence of all notes with each other is unavoidable, giving rise to true solidarity in the harmony of our human melody.

Quantum physics suggests that all possibilities we could experience and interpret as a linear sequence of lives and incarnations coincide. But, our individual temporal consciousness lets us see only one of those many experiences! Recent scientific superstrings theories suggest an additional number of dimensions surrounding us and that we cannot see or understand.

Therefore, reincarnation is an experience of the Ego, co-created by his ignorance, not understanding that what he reincarnates in the universe is God through his Children in an infinite multidimensional experience! (if you understand this, you've passed the final exam!)

I prefer to accept my co-responsibility in creating my experience, be it linear or multidimensional, adding my small contribution to the harmony of the great symphony of the universe. Likewise, we must break the codependent state the Ego binds us in, changing it

160

to a relationship of interdependence and solidarity with the universe and its infinite manifestations.

And now, fellow travelers, let us share our life's journey in solidarity by looking at the universe through the eyes of the Spirit.

BONUS QUESTIONS TO IMPROVE YOUR GRADE

1. Carefully study the concept of codependence in your life and see if you have experienced it in your relationships and upbringing. See how it has affected you and how you can correct it. Suggestions: Look for your failures, fears, failed relationships, dysfunctional upbringings, resentments, and experiences with the difficult people in your lives.

2. How can you use what you learned about your co-responsibility (free will) and co-creativity to correct the harmful aspects of codependent relationships in your life?

3. Review all the actions that have caused you guilt and suffering in your lives. Then evaluate the concept of forgiveness and the causal law of Love about these actions. Ask yourself:

   a) Who did you insult?

b) Why did you do it?

c) Who prosecutes and decides the consequence of your actions?

d) How can you fix it as quickly as possible?

e) Should you demand forgiveness for the acts of those who have caused you suffering?

4. Use the wise words of our Lord Jesus, "Father, forgive them because they do not know what they are doing" (Luke 23:43) and apply it to your acts and those of others in your lessons of the school of life.

REFLECTION AND MEDITATION EXERCISE

Continue with the previously recommended meditations, and try to bring a meditative status to your daily living through a state of alertness, in which you maintain your vision through the eyes of the Spirit.

Practice the human qualities of love, patience, empathy, tolerance, compassion, joy, and courage (perseverance) when facing the onslaught of your Ego.

Use previously suggested techniques of communication with the unloved (difficult persons), starting with your family and loved ones first and then extending your reach to others as you master your actions in your inner circle. Never forget to let yourself be loved openly at all times, because within you is the purest source of love!

THE RETURN TO THE GARDEN OF EDEN: REMEMBERING THE WAY BACK

THE MAP AND COMPASS THAT HELP US TO RETURN HOME – A BOOK SUMMARY

Glossary Chapter VIII

Compassionate Intelligence—When love guides our reasoning in the conviction of a holographic and solidarity universe, it produces the loving wisdom that characterized all great masters. These teachers learned to live in the world without attachment, because they recognized that their hearts never left the Kingdom of God.

Remembering the Way Back to Our True Home

In Chapter III we found that we forgot certain inherent qualities of our nature, with which we must remember to find the way back home and restore the existence of these characteristics. These are:

1. The ability to understand our origin.

2. The ability to know how these qualities interact.

3. The ability to understand how they influence our vision of life (happiness or suffering).

After the Self recognizes the existence of these characteristics, the yearning to return home resurfaces, which motivates us to find our path back.

The Garden of Eden: The Meaning of the Myth

The Garden of Eden is the myth of how the primordial love produces:

1. The mental duality and appearance of the existing universe and time with its infinite cycles.

2. Emotions, the classification of what exists as good or bad because of our attachment to happiness, and the rejection of suffering that generates the Ego and the loss of our innocence

3. The condition in which the consciousness of man existed in the Garden, described by ancient religions (BC) and by Judeo-Christianity as one purer and similar to the natural state of the "creator" of the universe, which was referred to as "heaven".

The Garden of Eden: The Symbolic Meaning

1. It represents the Golden Age of oriental traditions, where the Self lived in a state of innocence with minimal mental dualism and in the presence of creative divinity. It did not yet discern good from evil and lived in innocence while connected to its mother (God) by its umbilicus in her matrix (Garden of Eden).

2. The forbidden fruit represented the potential of discerning good and evil that the self was not yet ready to manage. It symbolized reason, rational intelligence, and the development of the five senses, which would allow humans to understand and organize the universe according to its universal laws. From this moment, the children of man begin to use their free will to co-create while learning from their mistakes.

3. The apple represents the potential knowledge that the Self can discover by classifying the world as good, bad, or indifferent. It is the development of the five senses at their maximum capacity, with the consequence (responsibility) of experiencing pleasure or suffering. It also symbolizes the emergence of intelligence, reason, and analysis and the ability to organize the universe with scientific laws created by the mind through habits and social customs. Finally, it represents the loss of innocence (irresponsibility or carelessness?) which leads to

the experience of time and cycles of birth, sickness, and death.

4. The Tree of Life represents the immortal potential of the Self when it realizes that time does not exist. This state of mindfulness is the wisdom that potentially exists in all children of man when they understand they can diversely manifest in the universal experience as Children of God, the Christ, or the Buddha. It is the final part of the cosmic journey, when the prodigal son returns to his Father's house, with the wisdom obtained during his human experience!

Two Lineages of the Self

1. The Prodigal Son (children of Man) - All of us in this world are like "prodigal sons". We ask for our human lineage, intelligence, and reason to use it responsibly in our universal experience, but we forget our true heritage and dedicate ourselves to living carelessly, as Frank Sinatra expressed in

169

the song, "My Way." These are the ones who live in selfishness. **Remember that living, if we do so with selfishness and lack of awareness of our interdependence with the laws of the universe and other beings, becomes a nightmare of suffering with brief moments of happiness.**

2. The Children of God (Spirit) – These people leave their father's house (the Garden of Eden) with a clear awareness of their true lineage, which is their spiritual inheritance based on love and the primordial state of the universe. **These are those who learn to look through the eyes of the Spirit and only see love around him. Yet, the only way to learn this is by living the earthly experience!**

Those who learned this lesson became the great Masters of all religions, such as Jesus, Buddha, Hermes, Moses, Krishna, Laotze, Muhammad, etc.

So, What Does Our Return to the Garden of Eden Represent?

1. It is the mental act of remembering what we have forgotten.

2. It is the reunion of our two natures (reconciliation, re-connection, or communion).

3. It is the act of learning to look at the universe anew, without prejudice or preconceptions (looking through the eyes of the Spirit).

4. It is forgiveness for ourselves and others.

5. It is meditation (communion or open bidirectional communication).

Which map should we use to return to paradise? This map is drawn from changes in our attitudes and actions that help us remember the way:

First, we must recognize that we are lost. This is the only requirement for taking this class. The compass to guide us on the correct path comes from meditation and prayer.

On the way back, we will meet many good Samaritans (the Masters) who have already made the journey and will help us stay on the right track.

Science and Reason Can Become Our Allies

Science helps us to find our origin when it teaches us, from observations that we have already discussed, that "Earthly life is just a mirage created by the thirst for individualism."

Reviewing what has already been covered, science suggests that 95% of the universe is invisible (antimatter). And that perceptible (matter), where we believe we exist, is the other 5%. Science can only understand and investigate this tiny perceivable part. We have previously discussed scientific theories that suggest the existence of more dimensions than the three we seem to understand, where time is a fictional creation of our mind, as Einstein proved with his theory of relativity.

Previously we postulated that everything perceptible is a temporary manifestation of the invisible universe. Examples include wind, light, thoughts, art, music, subatomic particles of matter, etc. We are beings originating from an immortal source (outside time and space), and we manifest transiently in time. If you still do not understand this, you are definitely going to flunk the final exam!

The Compass That Facilitates Our Journey

1. The compass takes us to a reunion of our two natures at the negotiating table (our hearts).

2. Initially, the Ego fights like a cornered cat, sticking to the five senses because it is afraid of losing control over the adopted children: the unloved ones. These are the selfish ones that really do not know what they are doing but

believe they know it all! They require lots of patience.

3. When the two minds meet at the negotiating table, it resembles when an orphaned child meets its lost mother and vice versa. Remember the song, *Love is more wonderful the second time around.*

4. The relative mind (material) is like a scratched vinyl record, which repeats the same message to us incessantly and does not let us hear the beautiful melody that resides in our hearts.

5. We finally realize that we have arrived at the Garden of Eden when the Self learns to look at the universe through the eyes of the Spirit and only finds love.

The Masters

These are the good Samaritans who, having found

their way, come back to help others find theirs. They also give us support and hope when we falter in our journey.

They have **Compassionate Intelligence** because their human experience in the universe of duality awakened the emphatic understanding that leads to compassion. This compassion is the Christian and Buddhist quality that the great teachers ask us to emulate.

By arriving and remembering our true nature, we feel part of something more inclusive, and not just individual and independent beings. Feeling like we are part of a great spiritual family makes us understand the phrase, "Love your neighbor as yourself" (Mathew 22:39).

Origin of Religious Discrepancies

Religious discrepancies happen because of the subjective limitation of the five senses and communication interference, which are not based on the teachings of the great Masters but rather on our personal interpretations.

Remember that divinity (the transcendent unifying force of the universe) is the unique universal broadcaster that only transmits love, unbiased to favorites.

And never forget the phrase of the Jewish Kabbalah, "The Name of God is so immensely great that it does not fit in my mouth."

The Power of Thought, Faith and Love

Thoughts move the energy of the universe, and the result depends on the intention. The more selfishness (individual desire) is involved, the worse the result is. **The best intention is a loving one, directing its purpose without intent!**

The intention is more effective the more evolution, awareness of solidarity, or spiritual wisdom there is in the action of thought.

176

Therefore, the pilot of our cosmic ship should be our inner wisdom (Children of God), not the Ego.

Faith is a **passively active** act of allowing the reconciliation of our dual nature, like religious communion. Faith occurs when the right ingredients are mixed in our hearts!

Negative emotions are like energetic roadblocks that obstruct the free circulation of our spiritual energy.

How Will We Know We Have Arrived at the Garden of Eden?

When arriving at the Garden of Eden, life takes such a satisfying perspective that all experiences taste just as good. We also obtain all the positive qualities that love can generate. We stop criticizing the world and let it be as it is, and then dedicate all our efforts to help others who have not yet remembered their origin.

And then, when we look in our backyard (heart), we realize that we never left our Garden of Eden!

BONUS QUESTIONS TO IMPROVE YOUR GRADE

1. Analyze and understand why God put the tree of knowledge in the Garden if he did not want his children to eat of its fruit. I would love to hear your answers!

2. What are the requirements to find (create) our maps?

3. Why is faith said to be a passively active act? Why not everything we believe we want with our minds becomes a reality in our lives?

4. List what you believe are the qualities of the Great Masters. Do you think you could acquire them at some point?

5. Describe in your own words what "Compassionate Intelligence" means. Look for opportunities to apply it in your lives. Give examples. Is this behavior compatible with the current business system? Look for government

systems that have tried to use Compassionate Intelligence in their political structure.

6. Remember some of the Good Samaritans who gave you something to quench your thirst on the journey. Remember how these actions affected you? Have you returned the favor to others?

REFLECTION AND MEDITATION EXERCISE

To remember our origin, we must learn to look through the eyes of the Spirit as we view the rest of the universe. For that, let's repeat the following meditation, mentioned previously in the book.

A Colorful Bath of Love

Sitting in a comfortable position with your back straight and head upright, visualize a source of spiritual strength or energy that makes you feel protected. For example, the figure of the Sacred Heart of Jesus, of youthful appearance, smiling and standing, with his arms open and emanating rays of multicolored light from the center of his heart to yours, where there is a small seed.

Understand the meaning of the exercise. Jesus represents the human manifestation of the Holy Spirit, which is the force of love left to us by God after his son left. The multicolored rays represent the infinite ways in which love could manifest itself among humans. The seed in your heart represents the possible way in which love resides in humans.

As these rays of light begin to fill your heart, feel loved and protected by the love of God, and watch as the little seed begins to open and, in turn, emanates the multiple colors of love everywhere. Imagine how those colors bathe you in love and reach all parts of our bodies, especially those where there is some discomfort or disease, and visualize how these aches and pains are pacified and healed.

After you feel fulfilled with joy and wellness, in gratefulness, share this meditation with all human beings, especially those who have hurt us in the past in their ignorance for not feeling loved.

Visualize multicolored rays that reflect from your heart towards all human beings, without distinction, including those who have left this world and those who, in your way of thinking, have brought suffering into your live. Dedicate a few minutes to this action and then rest your mind in silence for a few extra minutes. End the meditation giving thanks for this opportunity. Do this exercise every day when you get up and when you go to bed.

In the end, to keep your mind in a state of tranquility, imagine that your thoughts are like clouds in the sky and that your state of mind is like the stillness of the blue color of heaven. Let your thoughts pass as if they were clouds, without following them, and focus on the blueness of the sky, your natural state.

FINAL TEST

FOR THE SCHOOL OF LIFE

Instructions: choose the best answer

1. What is antimatter?

   a) A new socialist party that opposes rampant consumerism

   b) What produced matter according to science

   c) What occupies most of our universe (72%)

   d) What ghosts are made of

2. In what percentage of our potential universe do we perceive to exist?

   a) For most of us, nowhere!

b) In 5%

c) In 95%

d) None of the above

3. Einstein's Theory of Relativity might explain the following:

a) Puerto Rican custom to be late for appointments!

b) Why we never have enough time to finish the work assigned by the boss!

c) Reason why we think our high school classmates look older than ourselves!

d) Why time varies depending on where it is measured in the universe

4. The phrase "I think, therefore I am" was coined by:

a) Plato in The Republic

b) Isaac Newton in his Theory of Mechanical Physics

c) Rene Descartes, in his Theory of Rationalism

d) None of the above

5. The phrase "I am, therefore I think" was coined by:

a) Plato

b) Einstein

c) Isaac Newton

d) Iván Figueroa-Otero, MD

6. The holographic effect of the self within its universe is recognized in:

a) The biblical quotations "[...] *Truly I tell you, whatever you did for one of the least of these brothers and sisters of mine, you did for me.*"

(Mathew 25:40), and *"Love your neighbor as yourself."* (Mathew 22:39)

b) Global warming associated with human-made air pollution

c) Genetic alteration of agricultural products

d) All of the above

7. The Golden Law is:

a) The one that sorted the value of money by the planet's gold reserves

b) The one that sets the price of gold based on its weight

c) Do not do onto others what you do not like to have done to you

d) The rich always get away with it!

8. What are the highlights of creative co-responsibility?

a) Free will makes us co-responsible for the results of our actions

b) The most efficient way to manifest God's love in the universe is through the co-responsible actions of every child of God (human)

c) Planet Earth is our home, and what affects it affects all its children

d) All of the above

9. We can say the following about our DNA:

a) It came from monkeys

b) Each race emerged from a different one

c) It came from the stars, and produced all races

d) None of the above

10. The Energy Conservation Law:

a) Promotes the reduction of over-consumption of oil

b) Promotes adulteration of gasoline with alcohol to avoid alcoholism

c) Forces me to use regular gasoline instead of the premium one

d) Is the law of thermodynamics, where neither energy nor matter can be lost in the universe, since one transforms into the other

11. Qualities that characterize selfish people:

a) Their actions don't reflect regards for their effects on others

b) They promote individualism as opposed to interdependence

c) They live without transcendence, as their existence ends with the death of the physical body

d) All of the above

12. Only thing humans agree on is:

   a) That we like vegetarian cuisine

   b) That we all want to be happy

   c) That we want to be United States citizens

   d) That we will all go to heaven

13. What did Jesus imply on the cross by saying, "Father, forgive them because they do not know what they are doing" (Luke 23:43) when referring to those who killed Him?

   a) They did not recognize Jesus as a child of God

   b) They did not recognize they were also children of God

   c) They did not acknowledge they were Jesus' spiritual brethren

d) All of the above

14. Cosmic schizophrenia is:

a) A new form of mental illness that affects astronauts who spend a lot of time in space

b) What happens to astronauts when they eat a lot of junk food in space

c) What happens when mission control informs them that they do not have enough fuel left to return to Earth

d) Mental confusion where humans manifests a double personality, as Children of God or children of man, that makes them live in an unbalanced mental state and which brings much confusion and suffering

15. Shamata is:

a) A time-killing meditation technique

b) A deadly blow with the Samurai sword

c) A way to meditate with only one eye open

d) None of the above

16. What interference prevents humans from recognizing the whole of their reality?

   a) The limitation of perceiving the universe with the five senses

   b) Genetic heritage

   c) Habits and prejudices learned in our upbringing

   d) All of the above

17. What are the communication errors that can occur in the reception of the Great Broadcaster's signal?

   a) Interference in the individual interpretation (radio) caused by their personal experiences (parenting, education, race etc.)

b) Choosing the wrong station with your free will (metal rock instead of salsa!)

c) Interference created when relaying the received message to others

d) All of the above

18. The periodic table is:

a) A numerical reference to calculate the duration of the menstrual cycle

b) What the industry uses to periodically calculate employee layoffs!

c) How Mendelev classified items by groups of families with similar chemical characteristics

d) None of the above

19. We can say that learned habits and patterns of behavior are:

a) Good when we like them and bad when we do not like them

b) Relative to our form of parenting, race, nationality, social level, religious beliefs, and genetic heritage

c) The root cause of our social, political, and personal conflicts

d) All of the above

20. The real source of suffering is:

a) Humanity's social and economic inequality

b) Extreme capitalism

c) Governments' political corruption

d) The emptiness (lack of solidarity) that happens within us (cosmic schizophrenia) when we do not remember our true origin and the power of free will with love

21. The root of evil is:

a) Ignorance of the Ego by not recognizing its source of love (God)

b) Fear of aging, sickness and death due to ignorance, and the frustration, envy, and anger born from the fact that we cannot avoid these events

c) The selfish actions that lead humans to meet their individual needs first, regardless of the consequences for others

d) All of the above

22. We can say that free will:

a) Is the same for everyone

b) Happens only in democratic countries

c) Was made up by George Washington

d) Is the gift of love, which enables us to co-create responsibly

23. The first step to pass the final exam of life is to understand these abilities:

a) The ability to understand our origin

b) The ability to understand how our qualities interact

c) The ability to understand how these influence our vision of life (happiness or suffering)

d) All of the above

24. Which of these is the most effective quality in an act of loving and co-responsible co-creation?

a) Intelligence

b) Persistence

c) Prayer

d) Patience

25. Faith is:

a) An act of loving codependency with the creative force

b) A prayer based on certainty about the creative force that resides outside of us

c) Extreme reliance in love's ability to govern the universe in its own way (like Frank Sinatra)

d) An act of loving, patient responsible co-creation (knows how to wait for its turn on the universal waiting list)

26. What does the parable of the prodigal son teach us about the "nagging" we use with our children?

a) That no one learns from the experiences of others

b) That for the Father, spiritual inheritance is more valuable than the material one

c) That we, like the prodigal son, will learn to recognize our true heritage through the hardships of life

d) All of the above

27. About religions, we can say:

a) That they all have some of the truth

b) That none have the whole truth

c) That they make the mistake of creating God in their image and likeness

d) All of the above

28. What can humans use to escape from their self-made, five-sense prison of birth, aging, and death?

a) A drill made of love and faith

b) A drill made of free will and co-responsibility

c) The meditation drill

d) All of the above

29. Meditation is:

a) A passive action done in several very uncomfortable postures

b) Repeating sounds in strange languages

c) An open bidirectional communication, expressing oneself and listening

d) None of the above

30. To invite the Ego to the negotiating table (heart) you must:

a) Force it

b) Deceive it with promises of profit and power

c) Convince it with reason and the examples of personal experiences

and actions

d) All of the above

31. The worst punishment we can inflict on Latinos when they try to communicate is:

a) To call them "Hispanic"

b) Tell them they have no rhythm when dancing

c) Tie both arms down and force them to describe the last soccer game they saw

d) None of the above

32. Synonyms for the difficult people in our lives are:

a) Blind in spirit

b) Unloved

c) Spiritually lame

d) All of the above

33. What is the relationship that all difficult people like to establish with others?

    a) Totalitarian

    b) Supporting

    c) Codependence

    d) Interdependence

34. What are the difficult ones' most obvious characteristics?

    a) Poor self-esteem

    b) They hide their weakness with abusive preemptive attacks

    c) They do not know how to love or let themselves be loved

d) All of the above

35. Why are difficult people important in our lives?

   a) Because we are sadomasochists

   b) Because they take advantage of our naiveté
   (they make us think they are doing you a
   favor!)

   c) Because they allow us to practice the
   teachings of love so that they recognize love
   within themselves

   d) None of the above

36. Characteristics of open bidirectional
   communication:

   a) Visual attention and bodily gestures should
   reflect openness and attentiveness (to see
   with the eyes of the Spirit)

   b) Not letting our prejudices (individual habits)
   interfere with communication

c) Remembering that no one is right all the time and allowing ourselves to be wrong and learn from the perspectives of others

d) All of the above

37. Compassionate intelligence is when:

a) We are heartbroken and angry with the injustices that humans do to others

b) We allow others to mistreat us without taking revenge, even if we are bursting with rage

c) We learn to look at all beings with the eyes of the Spirit (heart)

d) None of the above

38. What does the return to the Garden of Eden mean?

a) It is the encounter of our two natures (reconciliation, connection, or communion)

b) It is learning to look at the universe without judgment and preconceptions (looking with the eyes of the spirit)

c) It is an act of forgiveness towards ourselves and others

d) All of the above

39. Why is forgiveness the most efficient way to demonstrate love in the universe?

a) Because by forgiving the actions of those who do not know what they do, we eliminate the need for the suffering created by our guilt.

b) Because forgiveness returns to us amplified in its healing of all my mistakes made in ignorance

c) Because "what is done to one of mine, they do to me"

d) All of the above

BIBLIOGRAPHY

BOOKS THAT HELPED ME CREATE MY VISION, DIRECTLY OR INDIRECTLY

- The Bible
- Khenchen Palden Sherab Rinpoche. *Door to Inconceivable Wisdom and Compassion.*
- Kenchen Palden Sherab Rinpoche *Opening to Our Primordial Nature.*
- Lao-Tzu. *Tao Te Ching.*
- Rabi Shimon bar Yojai. *The Zohar.*
- The Three Initiates. *The Kybalion.*
- Paramahansa Yogananda. *The Autobiography of a Yogi.*
- Plato, *The Dialogues.*
- Amit Goswami Ph.D. *The Self-Aware Universe.*
- Ken Wilder. *A Brief History of everything.*
- Chogyam Trungpa. *Cutting Through Spiritual Materialism.*

- M. Scott Peck. *The Road Less Traveled.*

- Hermann Hesse. *Siddhartha.*

- Shantideva. *The Guide to the Bodhisattva Way of Life.*

- Sogyal Rinpoche. *The Tibetan Book of Living and Dying.*

- Jerry Jampolsky. *Love Is Letting Go of Fear.*

- Richard Bach. *Illusions.*

- Helen Schucman. *A Course of Miracles.*

- Deepak Chopra. *Quantum Healing.*

- Khalil Gibran. *The Prophet.*

- Canonica, Franca. *The One Being* (6 volumes) www.elserunobooks.com

IVÁN FIGUEROA OTERO M.D.
FACS, FAAMA

After graduating from the School of Medicine of the University of PR, Dr. Figueroa-Otero trains as General Surgeon at the University Hospital of the UPR, integrating a one-year fellowship in cancer and one in experimental research and clinic. Post-graduate studies in Pediatric Surgery at Miami Children's Hospital and the Hospital of San Juan Municipal Hospital followed.

Looking for non-surgical or less invasive options for pediatric conditions, Dr. Figueroa-Otero explores Eastern philosophies that emphasize a holistic concept. He was one of the first physicians to become certified in medical acupuncture in Puerto Rico, training in traditional Chinese medicine and acupuncture with professors from the University of Seville. Eventually, he was certified in medical acupuncture nationwide.

207

In 2009, the Doctor got a certification in anti-aging medicine. In December of that year, he retired from pediatric surgery, focusing instead on a comprehensive medical practice and emphasizing disease prevention and modifying styles life.

In 2011 he was invited to become a Trustee of the American Board of Medical Acupuncture, which is the national body responsible for certifying physicians in the field of acupuncture through national exams. In that same year, he was recognized by *Natural Awakenings Magazine* as Holistic Physician of the Year.

Currently engaged in his private practice, Dr. Figueroa-Otero continues in his role as an educator, trying to achieve full integration of traditional Chinese acupuncture courses in the curriculum of medical schools, allowing physicians to be certified both locally and nationally, and to establish clinical research protocols on the use of acupuncture in known conditions compared to the methodology established by modern medicine. Another immediate priority is to incorporate meditation techniques and their role in preventive and therapeutic medicine.

Dr. Figueroa-Otero is the author of the School of Life trilogy, with the books *Spirituality 101: For the Dropouts of the School of Life*, *Spirituality 1.2: For the Disconnected from the School of Life*, and *Spirituality 103: The Key to Forgiveness, Finding the Light in Our Shadows*. He also published an abstract of his most important quotes titled *Spirituality 104: Reflections in my Magical Mirror*.

His books received awards from institutions like the Benjamin Franklin Award, NIEA Award, Readers Favorite, Beverly Hills Award, and USA Best Book Awards. They have also received excellent reviews by Focus on Women Magazine and the Kirkus Book Review, among others.

Currently, Dr. Figueroa-Otero is a commentator on his weekly television show, Needles Weaving Health, broadcasted on local Puerto Rico channel #27

(Liberty), #26 (Claro), and #8.1 (Antena). It is streamed on www.tivatv.com.

For more information, visit Dr. Figueroa-Otero's website at www.ivanfigueroaoteromd.com.

www.ingramcontent.com/pod-product-compliance
Lightning Source LLC
Chambersburg PA
CBHW060012050426
42448CB00012B/2712